Rosemary

From Maureen

— Mother's Day 1998 —

# THE FLOWER
# GARDEN

*A CREATIVE STEP-BY-STEP GUIDE TO*

# THE FLOWER
# GARDEN

Author
**Sue Phillips**

Photographer
**Neil Sutherland**

WHITECAP
BOOKS

This edition published in 1995 by
Whitecap Books Ltd., 351 Lynn Avenue
North Vancouver, B.C., Canada V7J 2C4
CLB 4138
© 1995 CLB Publishing, Godalming, Surrey, England
Printed in Singapore
ISBN 1-55110-283-8

## Credits

Edited and designed: Ideas into Print
Photographs: Neil Sutherland
Photographic location: Country Gardens at Chichester
Typesetting: Ideas into Print and Ash Setting and Printing
Production Director: Gerald Hughes
Production: Ruth Arthur, Sally Connolly, Neil Randles,
Karen Staff, Jonathan Tickner

## THE AUTHOR

**Sue Phillips** began gardening at the age of four, encouraged
by her grandfather, and had her first greenhouse at eleven,
where she grew a collection of cacti and propagated all
sorts of plants. After leaving school, she worked for a year
on a general nursery before studying horticulture at
Hadlow College of Agriculture & Horticulture, Kent for
three years. For the next five years, she was co-owner and
manager of a nursery in Cambridgeshire, before joining a
leading garden products company as Gardens Adviser.
This involved answering gardening queries, handling
complaints, writing articles and press releases, speaking at
gardening events and broadcasting for local radio. In 1984,
she turned freelance and since then she has contributed
regularly to various gardening and general interest
magazines and has appeared often on radio and TV
programs. She is the author of several published books.
She lives in a very windy village on the south coast of
England near Chichester and has a very intensively
cultivated quarter-acre cottage garden on solid clay, plus a
vegetable garden next door, which she looks after with
help from her husband and hindrance from a Persian cat.

## THE PHOTOGRAPHER

**Neil Sutherland** has more than 25 years experience in a
wide range of photographic fields, including still-life,
portraiture, reportage, natural history, cookery, landscape
and travel. His work has been published in countless books
and magazines throughout the world.

*Half-title page: Pelargoniums in traditional clay pots.*
*Title page: Planting up a container of summer color.*
*Copyright page: A color-theme border in red and purple.*

# CONTENTS

# Introduction

# THE VALUE OF FLOWERS

Flowers are not just the window dressing of the garden; for most people, they are the single most important ingredient. Fortunately, there are plenty of them. There are flowers to grow for traditional herbaceous borders and in containers or in creative schemes, such as flower lawns and carpet bedding displays. There are flowers for cutting and flowers for extreme conditions, ranging from boggy soil through shade to hot sun. And the way to have plenty of color is to grow as many different kinds of flowers as possible - all year round.

The season starts with winter-flowering iris and hellebores, moving on to dwarf bulbs, such as snowdrops and *Iris reticulata*. These are followed by spring bedding, such as polyanthus and wallflowers, all the popular spring bulbs including daffodils and tulips, plus early-flowering perennials, such as *Brunnera* and *Pulmonaria*. Summer is no problem - annual bedding plants, roses and a huge range of herbaceous perennials take care of that. Later-flowering dahlias and chrysanthemums, Japanese anemones and *Sedum spectabile* follow on, until finally colchicums, fall crocus and kaffir lily *(Schizostylis)* join forces with fall foliage tints to bring the season to a colorful close.

However, flowers alone do not make a garden. It is the way the plants are put together that makes a garden truly memorable. That, and the ability to pick the right flower for a given situation - and give it the right attention just when it is needed - this creative input is what turns a collection of flowers into a garden. This book tells you how to do just that - whatever the problems your garden can throw at you.

*Left: The best mixed flower beds feature a variety of color, shape and height.* **Right:** *Tulips in glazed pots.*

# Preparing the soil

Before planting or sowing any flowers, it is essential to get the soil in good condition. If left unimproved - hard, lumpy and short of organic matter or plant nutrients - flowers will take a long time to become established and will not grow or bloom as well as they should. Basic soil preparation involves digging, feeding and creating a fine surface ready for planting or sowing. To improve the structure and water-holding capacity of the soil, spread organic matter, such as well-rotted garden compost, manure, etc., over the soil and dig it in. This creates air spaces by 'fluffing' up the soil. Digging is traditionally done in the fall, when annual weeds and organic matter can be turned into the soil, allowing the soil bacteria to have the whole winter to 'digest' anything that is not totally decomposed. Be sure to remove perennial weeds when digging; if they are a real problem, treat them with weedkiller to eradicate them completely. If digging is not done in the fall, do it in spring, several weeks before planting, but add only very well decomposed organic matter. In spring and early summer, a few days before planting, fork the ground over roughly to loosen soil that has been flattened by winter rain, etc, and remove any weeds. Then make the final pre-planting or sowing preparations. First comes feeding. Sprinkle a general fertilizer over the ground at the manufacturer's suggested rate for pre-planting. Then rake to mix this with the soil, remove any surface stones and lumps, and produce a fine crumblike finish in which small plants and seeds can 'get away' quickly. Avoid treading on the soil again after it has been prepared.

*1 Spread a layer of well-rotted organic matter (this is manure) over the soil. It should be at least 1-2in(2.5-5cm) deep.*

## Preparing for planting

*1 When the soil has been dug over, improved and left for the winter, the next stage is to fork it over to loosen it. Break down clods by hitting them with the prongs.*

*2 Sprinkle fertilizer over the area, taking care to spread it evenly. Always follow the manufacturer's instructions regarding the rate at which to use the fertilizer.*

*3 Rake the fertilizer well into the top 1in(2.5cm) of soil. Take this opportunity to remove any small stones and other debris that have come to the surface.*

*4 Sprinkle an inorganic fertilizer or an organic feed, such as fish, blood and bone, evenly over the soil at the manufacturer's suggested rate.*

*2 Dig the ground over to the full depth of the spade, turning each sod so that the organic matter is buried beneath the surface.*

*3 Rake the soil to break down clods, and remove any roots or stones, leaving it roughly level. Allow the area to lie fallow for the winter.*

Peat. Choose sphagnum moss peat for acid beds. Sedge peat has been largely superseded by cheaper, environment-friendly alternatives for general soil improvement.

Coir. Spent coir mix or natural coir (coconut fiber) is an environment-friendly alternative to peat, but expensive to use for soil improvement unless no other source of bulky organic matter is available.

Well-rotted horse manure. Useful source of bulky organic matter, but not an alternative to fertilizer. Use both.

Spent growing bag soil. After one season's use, growing tomatoes, etc., the nutrients will be exhausted but the soil is a good source of organic matter for the garden.

Fish, blood and bone fertilizer. A general-purpose organic feed for use before planting and for sprinkling between plants every 6 to 8 weeks during the growing season.

*5 Finally, rake the soil once more to mix the fertilizer into the top 1in (2.5cm) of soil and leave a fine tilth.*

Home-made garden compost. This is the result of piling damp annual weeds, grass clippings and household peelings, etc, in a compost bin for 6 to 12 months until it resembles soil.

Pea shingle. Dig in at 1-2 bucketsful per square yard/ meter to improve surface drainage of heavy clay soil. Or apply as decorative mulch.

A balanced inorganic fertilizer, one of the cheapest general-purpose feeds available. Use as described for fish, blood and bone.

# Sowing seeds directly in the garden

The time-saving alternative to sowing seed in pots, pricking out and then planting, is to sow straight into the garden soil. This way, there is no need to buy pots, trays or seed-sowing mixture, so it is a far cheaper way to produce plants. It is mainly used for hardy annuals, such as cornflower, clarkia, godetia, etc., as these can be sown outdoors in early spring to start flowering in early summer. Half-hardy annuals, such as French marigolds, cannot be sown outside until after the last frost and would not start flowering till the end of summer. For direct sowing, it is essential to have good, well-prepared soil that is free of weed seeds, otherwise you will not be able to tell the flowers from the weeds - they all look similar as seedlings. Two methods are used for sowing seed straight into garden soil. One is to scatter the seed over well-dug and raked soil, where you want them to flower. Seed of several different kinds of flowers can be sown in adjacent groups, marked out in advance with a trickle of sand. For this to work, you must have soil with no weed seeds whatever, which is rarely possible. The second, and better, method is to sow seeds thinly in rows in a spare patch of well-prepared soil (perhaps the vegetable garden), thin the seedlings to 1-2in(2.5-5cm) apart, then transplant them to the flower bed. The second method is also useful for sowing hardy biennials, such as wallflowers, canterbury bells and polyanthus, and herbaceous flowers (delphiniums, etc.) sown in early summer and transplanted in early fall.

*1 Prepare the ground, then trickle silver sand to mark out patterns on the soil. Mix long, narrow shapes with blocky and tapering 'teardrop' shapes for a Persian carpet-like effect.*

*2 Sprinkle seed by hand, taking care not to overlap the edges of each shape. Adjacent patches should have contrasting colors and flower shapes, with taller kinds to the back or center.*

*3 When the whole bed has been sown, rake it very gently, barely disturbing the soil, so that you work the seeds into the surface of the soil. The sandy lines should disappear, too.*

## Sowing seeds for later transplantation

*1* Prepare the soil well and make a depression 0.5in(1.25cm) deep with the edge of a hoe. Sprinkle seeds thinly along it.

*2* Cover the seeds with a thin scattering of soil using the rake very gently along the depression, until it is barely filled with soil particles.

*3* Label the row with the name of the seed sown and date. Water well, using a fine rose, so that the soil is evenly moistened, not flooded.

*4* Water the bed very thoroughly, so that the seeds and soil surrounding them are evenly damped. Use a fine rose to prevent the seed being washed away from their correct place.

Agrostemma milas

Coreopsis 'Special Mixture'

**Right:** Agrostemma, coreopsis *and* godetia *sown directly into weed-free border soil where the plants are to flower. If seedlings come up too thickly they can be thinned, but a dense stand of flowers adds to the whole effect.*

Godetia 'Sybil Sherwood'

# Raising seed in trays

**1** *Slightly overfill the tray with loose seed-sowing mixture and strike the excess off level with a flat piece of wood, leaving the surface roughly level.*

*A peat-based mix is fine for raising these seeds.*

**2** *Lightly firm the surface with the base of a clean flowerpot or wooden 'presser'. Leave the mixture level and about 0.25in(6mm) below the rim.*

**3** *Tip the seeds into a piece of folded paper. To sow them, tap the paper gently, so that the seed is thinly and evenly distributed over the surface of the seed-sowing mixture. These are Nigella, or love-in-a-mist.*

If you need many plants of the same type, it pays to sow a whole packet of seed into a tray, as this will produce enough seedlings to prick out four to six trays of plants. If you share the job of plant raising with friends or neighbors and swap your spare trays of plants, it saves everyone buying several packets of seed - a good idea when you consider that flower seed germinates best in the year you buy it. Sow seeds as thinly and evenly as possible - imagine each seed turning into a small plant - and prick out the seedlings as soon as they are large enough to handle. If you are sowing medium to large flower seeds, you can avoid the job of pricking out seedlings altogether by sowing directly into small individual containers, such as 2in(5cm) pots or 'cells' (small honeycomb-like modules). Since only about 50% of flower seeds germinate, sow two medium-sized or one large seed per small container, to allow for failures. As the volume of potting mixture is so small in these tiny 'cells' they dry out very quickly, so regular watering is vital. Standing them on damp capillary matting on a greenhouse bench helps. Young plants are ready for planting out when the containers are completely filled with roots. To remove them from their 'cells', water them the day before so that the seed mix is just firm, and lift them out with a small pickle fork.

**4** *Cover the seeds to their own depth with more of the same seed mixture. Use a kitchen sieve to ensure an even covering of fine material free from lumps.*

## Sowing large seeds in small pots

**1** *You can sow large nasturtium seeds singly into small pots. Fill each pot with seed-sowing mix and press one seed into the middle.*

**2** *This avoids pricking out, as each plant is self-contained in its own pot. When the pots are filled with root, plant them out.*

**5** *Label the tray with the plant name and date. Water the seed tray by standing it in a dish of tepid water. When the surface of the seed mix turns a darker color, you know that it is wet right through.*

**6** *Remove the seed tray from the water and cover it with a transparent lid. If you do not have a lid, slip the tray into a large, clear plastic bag with a couple of short sticks inside to lift the plastic up like a tent.*

## Medium seeds in cells

**1** *To fill the cells, pile seed-sowing mix loosely on top of the module and smooth it out evenly, making sure the cells around the edge are well filled.*

**2** *Make a shallow depression in the middle of each cell and drop in two seeds. Sow only as many of one variety as you need plants, plus a few spare seeds.*

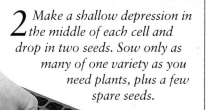

*These are the seeds of Convolvulus.*

**3** *Cover the seeds by sieving enough seed mix over the cells to fill the depressions and bury the seed with roughly their own depth of mix.*

**4** *Water well in with a fine rose on a watering can. This also helps to firm the soil. If you need to move the tray, slide a sheet of thin board under the cells.*

**5** *Do not expect total germination; in many cases, only one of the two seeds will come up. Thin out any 'doubles' to leave only the strongest seedling.*

*1* Fill clean 3.5in(9cm) pots with seed-sowing mixture. Tip the seeds (these are French marigold) into a fold of paper and scatter thinly over the surface.

# Raising seed in pots

Although garden centers offer quite a good selection of flowers in bloom and ready to plant, it is much more satisfying to grow your own right from the start. Mail-order seed catalogs offer a far larger range of flower varieties to grow at home, including unusual ones that you may not be able to buy as plants. And, particularly if you want many plants of the same kind, raising your own can be far cheaper. Some kinds of flowers can be sown straight into the garden (see page 14), but half-hardy annuals must be sown early on in reasonable warmth if they are be in flower by the start of summer. Sow these in pots under controlled conditions. If you intend raising many plants, it is best to use an electrically heated propagator inside a frost-free greenhouse. This way you not only have the means of maintaining the right temperature for the seeds to germinate (60-75°F/15-24°C depending on the type), but you will also have room to grow them on when the seedlings are pricked out into trays. If you only need a few plants, then use warm windowsills around the house. Choose shady sills for pots of seed that are germinating, as direct sun can harm them. Then when the seedlings are pricked out, move them to a brighter spot after a few days so that they do not become drawn up and spindly. If space is short and you only need a few plants of each kind, it is not essential to prick seedlings out into trays at all - instead just plant them straight into small pots - these are likely to fit better onto a windowsill.

*2* If the seeds are very fine, sprinkle a thin layer of vermiculite over the surface before sowing them.

*3* Tip the fine seed (here petunia) into a fold of paper and scatter it thinly and evenly over the vermiculite. Seeds fall between the particles and do not need covering.

*4* Cover medium-sized and large seeds to their own depth with sieved seed mix. Use a clean flowerpot with small holes in the base if you do not have a sieve.

*5* Stand the pots in a dish containing a few inches of tepid water until the surface of the soil turns dark, showing that it is wet right through.

**Right:** *French marigolds are robust and long-flowering. Plant them out when they are already starting to bloom. Deadhead regularly.*

**Below:** *Petunias have large, fragile blooms that need a well-sheltered spot to keep them looking their best, especially if grown in a tall container.*

*The plastic bag helps to create a humid atmosphere.*

**6** Put the pots into individual clear plastic bags and secure them with rubber bands. Place on a warm windowsill (about 70°F/21°C)) in good light but out of direct sun.

## Removing seedlings

Prick out seedlings while they are tiny to give them more space to develop. Water the pot well the day beforehand. The seedlings in this pot are petunias

**1** Use a dibble, the tip of a pencil or a similar implement to 'tease' the seedlings gently apart. This becomes harder to do without damage if the seedlings are left in the pot too long.

**2** Hold the seedlings by a leaf, not the stem, as you transfer them to a clean tray filled with fresh seed potting mixture. Use a dibble to make holes in the mix.

**3** Lower individual seedlings into the evenly spaced prepared holes until the bottom leaves lie just above surface of the soil. Gently firm the roots in with the dibble.

**4** When the whole tray has been filled with seedlings, water them in using a fine rose on a watering can. Water again when necessary; keep the soil moist but not overwatered.

19

# Pelargonium cuttings

Taking cuttings is the quickest and easiest way to grow new plants of some kinds of flowers, notably half-hardy perennials, such as pelargoniums, fuchsias, argyranthemums, gazanias, etc. This group includes some plants that are treated as annuals, such as petunias and coleus, so use cuttings to increase your favorite colors from seed-raised plants. Cuttings taken any time between late spring and late summer root easily. From a practical point of view, it is a good idea to root cuttings in late summer so that small young plants can be kept on a windowsill indoors or under heated glass for the winter, where they take up less room than old plants. However, as long as they have enough warmth, cuttings taken in early spring will grow quickly and provide plants just coming into flower in time to plant out after the last frosts. This is the time to propagate plants you want to increase quickly. No special facilities are needed to root such easy cuttings; they will grow in a pot on a warm windowsill. Cuttings with thin leaves are best slipped inside a large loose plastic bag until they root, as it is vital to keep the air round them humid, otherwise they may die before they root. Thick, fleshy-leaved plants, and those with hairy, felty or gray or silver leaves, are best left uncovered, as too much humidity may make them rot.

*1* *Select and remove a young shoot 4-6in(10-15cm) long. If possible, take one without a flower, but with very free-flowering plants this may not be possible. This is a pelargonium.*

*2* *Use a sharp knife to remove the lower leaves. Make sure the blade is not in line with your thumb so that you cannot cut yourself. Otherwise cut down against a board.*

*3* *Remove any developing buds and flowers in the same way. By this time, the cutting will have just two or three leaves at the top and several inches of clean stem.*

*4* *Make a clean cut across the base of the stem just below a node, or leaf joint. This is where the new roots will emerge. Ragged tissue left here would rot.*

*5* *Dip the base of each cutting in rooting powder as an extra precaution. This contains fungicide as well as plant hormones to assist with the formation of a healthy, strong root system.*

**6** Push individual cuttings into a 2in (5cm) pot of seed sowing mix, or put a few cuttings 1.5in(3.75cm) apart around the edge of a 4in(10cm) pot.

**7** Water the cuttings in to settle the soil around the base of each stem, then allow to drain thoroughly. Keep just moist until properly rooted.

**8** When well rooted, after six to eight weeks, cuttings will start to make new growth and roots may be visible through the holes in the base of the pot. Tip cuttings out for potting.

Although it seems a shame to do so, remove any flowers from cuttings when potting them to allow more strength to go into the young plant.

**9** Separate each young plant, teasing the roots gently apart. Remove surplus old soil, leaving only that which surrounds the base of the plant and encloses the roots.

**10** Pot each cutting individually into a pot with fresh potting mixture, choosing a pot big enough to take all the roots and surrounding old soil with a little room to spare.

21

# Argyranthemum cuttings

Half-hardy perennials, such as pelargoniums, fuchsias and argyranthemums, are killed by freezing, so to propagate them, take cuttings from them in late summer. The young plants remain virtually dormant during the winter, needing just enough water to prevent shriveling. By spring, they will have filled the old pot with roots. Pot them on into fresh potting mixture and slightly larger pots and nip out the growing tips of the shoots to encourage branching. With regular feeding and watering, you will have good bushy plants ready to put outside by the time the last frost is past. If you should need to salvage old plants for the following year, dig them up just before the first fall frosts, shake the soil from the roots and cut back the top of the plant, leaving only a few inches of stem. Plant the roots individually into pots large enough to take them with some space to spare, and keep them in a heated greenhouse for the winter with a minimum of watering. Take the new shoots that appear in spring for cuttings to replace the old plants. If no heated facilities are available, try digging up the old plants, shaking off the soil and old leaves and hanging them up in netting in the roof of a dry, frost-free shed. However, it is better to buy a few new plants in spring and take cuttings from them in early summer, or buy a tray of cheap, rooted cuttings or seedlings to grow on at home.

*1 Propagate from your best plants if possible. They should be healthy, bushy and have flowered well. Cut off 3-4in(7.5-10cm) from the tips of, ideally, non-flowering shoots.*

*2 If suitable material is short, you may have to use some flowering shoots. With these, rooting is less certain, so take a few extra cuttings.*

*3 Collect the cuttings into a plastic bag and prepare them as soon as possible to avoid wilting. First, strip away the leaves from the bottom half of each shoot.*

*Use a seed-sowing soil mix*

*Fungicidal hormone rooting powder*

*Half-hardy perennials, such as these argyranthemums, are easy to propagate during late spring and summer.*

## Flowering shoots

With some kinds of plants that are particularly free-flowering and bloom continuously all summer, it is virtually impossible to find non-flowering shoots to use as cuttings. In this case, it is probably best to take one plant as a mother plant, cut it down hard and use the resulting flush of vigorous shoots as cuttings.

**1** When preparing cuttings made from flowering shoots, proceed as before, but take care to remove any flowers and developing buds, however tiny, as these will sap the strength of the new shoot.

Cut the stem off cleanly with a sharp knife.

**2** Removing a flower from the tip of a shoot may leave an odd-shaped cutting. As long as there are several normal leaves or a strong side shoot lower down, it is still usable.

**3** It is especially vital to give cuttings that have flowered a good start. Dip the base of the prepared cutting into rooting powder. Use a fresh tub of powder, as it loses its potency after six months.

**4** Dip the base of each cutting into fungicidal hormone rooting powder to prevent fungus infection and to stimulate the cut end to produce roots.

**5** Loosely fill 3.5in(9cm) pots with seed sowing mix and press a single cutting into the center of each one. Firm the soil lightly around it.

**6** When all the cuttings are in their pots, water them in lightly, so that the soil is thoroughly dampened and settled around the stems. Do not allow it to dry out. Expect rooting to take about six weeks.

# Routine maintenance

Flower gardens need regular care to keep them looking their best. Being small, flowers are soon overgrown by weeds if neglected, and because their foliage generally covers the ground, it is not very practical to use weedkillers between them, so a certain amount of hard work is necessarily involved. In early spring when much of the soil is bare, remove any weeds and mulch the exposed soil with a layer of well-rotted garden compost or manure about 1-2in (2.5-5cm) thick. This helps to retain moisture later, and also prevents the germination of annual weed seedlings. Leave areas planted with bulbs and spring bedding until later, when the foliage has died down or been removed. By late spring, herbaceous plants will be coming through.

**Below:** *With herbaceous flowers, such as* Incarvillea, *cut off the dead flower stems at the base to keep the bed tidy. It may also encourage further flowers.*

Protect the shoots from slugs, and support plant stems so that they grow straight. Hoe shallowly to remove weeds while they are tiny, and sprinkle fertilizer evenly around the plants. Individual plants known to be heavy feeders benefit from extra liquid feeds: clematis, for example, enjoy a liquid tomato feed in spring.

After the last frost is past in your area, plant out frost-tender bedding plants. Continue hoeing and feeding throughout the summer. If the weather is very dry, give newly planted flowers and annuals a good soaking every few days, rather than light waterings more often, and water in the evenings, especially in hot weather, to give plants plenty of time to take up the water before the next morning's sun causes it to evaporate. As summer moves on, regularly remove dead flowerheads and stalks to keep beds tidy. Sometimes, this also encourages further buds to form, as plants cannot then set seed. By fall, much of the dead foliage can be removed, leaving fall flowers to be seen at their best. Leave seedheads, such as teasel, until the husks have been emptied; they provide welcome seed for wild birds.

**Above:** *Deadheading roses. When the flowers are over, use secateurs and cut back 4-6in(10-15cm) below the flower, cutting just above a leaf joint.*

**Right:** *If roses are susceptible to disease, spray them regularly during the growing season with a rose fungicide, following the instructions.*

*1 Feed flowers regularly during the growing season from spring to midsummer. Sprinkle a good general fertilizer between the plants.*

**1** *Soon after lavender flowers have faded, reshape the plant by clipping the plants over to remove the dead heads and flower stems.*

**2** *Continue clipping round the plant to remove the tips of the young growth, taking care not to cut back into the old wood.*

**3** *Round off the 'shoulders' to make a neat, even bun shape. Clear away all the cuttings to avoid fungal infections building up.*

**4** *The finished effect seems rather artificial, but new sideshoots sprout within a few weeks, giving the plants a more natural look.*

*Use a fine spray and keep it just for pesticides. Never use it for weedkiller as well.*

**Right:** *Remove weeds such as this groundsel before they can shed seed. The easiest way to dig out individual weeds or those growing amongst other plants is with a small weeding fork.*

*When weeding, try to dig out the entire plant complete with its roots.*

**2** *Hoe in thoroughly but shallowly to ensure that the fertilizer is evenly mixed with the soil, without damaging plant roots.*

**3** *Water in very well after feeding to dissolve the feed and make it available to plants. In prolonged dry spells, give liquid feeds instead.*

# Pests and diseases

The odd outbreak of plant pests or diseases can occur in even the best kept garden. Many problems can be avoided by keeping weeds under control and tidying away rubbish. Compost lawn mowings, dead leaves and weeds so that they break down without encouraging pests or disease spores. Remove and burn plants with persistent problems. Wash empty pots, seed trays and boxes after use and store them in a shed. Natural predators will deal with many pests, so plant trees to encourage insect-eating birds, grow clumps of wildflowers to encourage beneficial insects, and avoid chemical pesticides so that beneficial creatures are not harmed. However, if a pest or disease problem is serious, use a remedy in order to save the plant. Even then it is not always necessary to resort to chemicals. Use physical barriers round plant stems; bury small gauge wire mesh over bulbs when planting them to deter burrowing creatures from eating them, and turn vacant ground over in winter so that birds can feed on soil pests. If chemical sprays are unavoidable, choose an environmentally friendly one where possible, and spray in the evening when bees are not about.

*Concentrated soft soap (natural fatty acids). Dilute with water and apply with hand-operated sprayer as a pesticide.*

*Ready-to-use sulfur spray, an organic remedy for mildew on roses, etc.*

*Slug tape impregnated with metaldehyde*

**Left:** *Aphids are very common garden pests; wait for bluetits and beneficial insects to clear minor outbreaks or use a chemical that only kills aphids.*

*Liquid slug killer*

*Slug pellets*

*Slugs slide off this nonstick barrier tape*

**Left:** *Roses are very prone to fungal diseases such as blackspot and rust (shown here). Spray regularly in spring and summer with a proper rose fungicide, or grow disease-resistant varieties.*

**Right:** *Leaf miner is a difficult insect to tackle as it lives inside the leaf itself. Spray with a systemic insecticide when you first see its trails.*

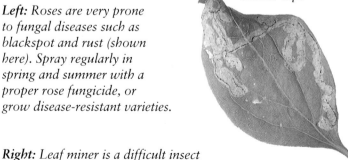

*Beneficial insect lures attract ladybugs, lacewings, etc. that feed on insect pests and their eggs.*

**Below:** *Slug and snail damage is worse in a damp season. If you can catch the culprits red-handed at night with the aid of a torch, it is possible to remove them without resorting to slug pellets.*

## Biological control

*Each white scale on this fuchsia leaf harbors an immature whitefly that will emerge like a tiny white moth. The black scales show where the parasitic wasp, Encarsia, has laid its eggs, killing the larval whitefly and producing a new generation of Encarsia.*

*Green sulfur protects stored bulbs from rots and mold.*

**Below:** *Powdery mildew on roses. Spray regularly with a fungicide. Cover the whole plant evenly on both upper and undersides of the leaves even if you are using a systemic product. Do not spray in hot sun, in windy conditions, or when the plants are under stress.*

**Below:** *Clematis with earwig damage to the flowers, and slug and snail damage on the leaves. Clear away any debris from nearby, and use slug tape or nonstick barrier tape around the base of the plant.*

*Clematis flower showing typical earwig damage.*

*Hormone rooting powder with fungicide.*

*Ammonium sulfate granules - slug remedy.*

# Instant gardening using annuals

For instant color almost anywhere, annuals are the answer. They are the simple solution for the new homeowner who wants a garden in a hurry, or for making an existing garden look its best for a special occasion. They are good for filling odd gaps in a border, for planting up containers and perfect for a balcony, patio or pathway. Annuals can also be used creatively in traditional knot gardens - or for Victorian-style carpet bedding schemes now enjoying a revival. They are also good value for planting in beds of their own where you need a splash of color that will last all summer. Use annuals in informal 'random-look' cottage-style planting schemes, or in formal beds edged with straight rows of flowers and blocks of color broken up by occasional 'dot' plants - perhaps standard fuchsias. However, annual beds are a lot of work, so do not take on more than you can comfortably manage. Plants can be grown from seed on warm windowsills indoors, or bought ready to plant from garden centers in early summer, just as they are coming into flower. Do not plant them out until after the last frost. Annuals need good soil and a sunny situation with reasonable shelter to do well. To keep plants flowering continuously they need frequent attention - watering, feeding and deadheading regularly. Since the plants do not survive freezing, pull them out in the fall and replace them with spring bulbs or winter and early spring bedding, to avoid leaving the beds empty.

**Above:** *Use annuals to fill a narrow bed that would soon be overcrowded if planted with perennials. These are antirrhinums, tuberous begonias, lobelia and dwarf African marigolds.*

**Right:** *A colorful knot garden using* Impatiens *to fill in the intricate patterns created by dwarf box hedges; A useful scheme for a shady spot as both kinds of plants are shade-tolerant.*

## Annuals in containers

Tubs, troughs and hanging baskets are the perfect way of decorating a patio and for adding eye-catching detail to special places all around the garden. Favorite plants include pelargoniums, fuchsias, begonias and lobelias, but almost any compact or trailing annual is suitable. Most annuals are sun lovers and need direct sun for at least half the day. Begonia semperflorens, Impatiens *and* fuchsias will flower in light shade if they are in flower when planted. The best time to plant up containers is in early summer, just after the last frost. Fill the pots with any good potting mix, remove the plants from their containers and plant them close together so that the pots look well filled from the start. Containers need daily watering; allow the potting mix to take up as much water as it can.

*Right:* A pot of Begonia semperflorens *will be a blaze of color all summer. It can be easily moved to different spots and looks good on an outdoor table, too.*

*Below:* Large containers suit a bold, mixed planting scheme. Here, verbena, pelargoniums and African marigolds make a striking and colorful display.

*Above:* Hardy annuals (Nigella, Calendula *marigolds and cornflowers) grown by the 'sow where they are to grow' method, make a distinct pattern in the floral carpet covering the bed.*

1 Prepare the soil over the entire bed some time in advance of planting. Dig a hole for each plant about twice the size of its rootball.

2 Put the excavated soil next to the hole, ready for filling in around the roots once the plant is in place.

3 Put a spadeful of well-rotted manure or other organic matter in the hole and mix well. Add more manure to the excavated soil.

# Planting a perennial

Perennial plants will stay in the same ground for two to four years, so it is vital to spend time on soil preparation before planting. Tackle soil pests with a soil insecticide or dig the ground several times in winter to expose pests to the birds. Dig in as much bulky organic matter as possible, sprinkle a general fertilizer evenly over the soil and rake it in shortly before planting. Perennial plants are traditionally planted in fall or early spring, but since they are dormant at that time, you may prefer to delay planting until mid-spring when some growth is visible. Buying pot-grown plants enables you to add new plants in summer when they are in full flower, but they will need generous watering during dry spells for the rest of that season to allow the roots to establish. Herbaceous perennials spread to form dense, congested clumps, with unproductive old material in the center and young flowering shoots only around the edge. After two to four years, split up the clump and throw away all the old exhausted central parts, leaving only young material, divided into fist-sized sections, to be replanted. The best time to do this is in early spring, just before the new flush of growth starts. A few of the more rugged types, such as michaelmas daisies, can be divided in the fall when the last flowers are over, but bearded irises need to be lifted and divided in summer, about six weeks after the flowers are over. Take this opportunity to improve the soil again before replanting and be sure to replant the clumps at the same depth as before. This is important: herbaceous peonies, for example, will not flower if their crown is planted more than 1in(2.5cm) below the soil surface, and bearded iris need planting so that the top half of each horizontal rhizome is above ground or they will suffer from the same problem.

4 Sprinkle a handful of general purpose fertilizer into the hole and mix well with the soil. Add half a handful of fertilizer to the pile of soil alongside the hole and, again, mix well.

**5** *Tip the plant gently out of its pot (knock the base of the pot sharply against something solid if the plant is difficult to dislodge). Slide the plant out without breaking up the rootball.*

**6** *Lift the plant by its rootball into the hole. Do not handle the plant by its stems. The top of the rootball should lie roughly level with the soil surface. Rotate the plant until its best side faces the front of the bed.*

**7** *Surround the rootball with the improved soil excavated from the planting hole, and firm it lightly down. Add more soil to bring it up to the level of the surrounding bed.*

**8** *Water well in, trickling water around the edge of the root-ball. Mulch with 1-2in (2.5-5cm) of rotted organic matter or bark chips and keep well watered.*

# Traditional herbaceous borders

The traditional English country house herbaceous border is long and narrow and backed by a yew hedge that provides a green background. The border is generously filled with a wide selection of flower shapes, sizes and colors, all apparently randomly mixed. (In fact, it needs careful planning to ensure that contrasting shapes are put next to each other and that colors are evenly distributed throughout the bed.) Since only herbaceous plants are used, the border looks bare in winter, but by choosing plants carefully it is possible for a big border to look good from spring to the fall. (If the border is small, aim for midsummer interest mainly, to avoid seasonal gaps.) Although the effect is stunning, a traditional herbaceous border takes a lot of looking after. Tall plants such as delphiniums must be staked, as the hedge creates shade that draws plants up, causing weak stems. The hedge also harbors weeds, pests and diseases, as well as taking moisture out of the soil, so the flowers need spraying, generous mulching and frequent hoeing for good results. The hedge also needs clipping. Yew only needs cutting once a year, so this can be done before the border grows up. However, a faster growing hedge needs cutting several times during the season. In this case, leave an access path at least three feet wide (about 1m) between the hedge and the back of the border. If space allows, it is not a bad idea to leave room for a path anyway, as this makes routine work like mulching, hoeing and weeding much easier as you can reach into the bed from both sides without treading on the soil.

*Above:* A traditional mixed border, with a clipped conifer hedge forming a leafy backdrop, and a profusion of perennials growing in amongst each other in a wild mixture of colors.

*Left:* Lupins bloom in early summer. Cut them down hard after flowering as they sometimes produce a second flush of flowers. They need sunny, well-drained soil.

# Island beds

An island bed is an informal-shaped bed cut into the lawn where you can walk right round it. It can be any shape you like; have one large bed or make a group of several smaller ones. Island beds are usually planted with the tallest plants in the middle and progressively shorter ones round the edge, so they look good from all angles. As the plants receive light from all round, their stems are stronger and need less staking. Being stronger, the plants suffer less from pests and diseases. Routine chores are easier, as you can reach plants from the lawn. Put

**Above:** *Island beds blend in well with a more informal garden.*

in traditional herbaceous plants and lilies but choose compact modern varieties. Or try using ornamental grasses and summer flowering bulbs.

**Below:** *Equally traditional is the double fronted border, which has a path between two borders face to face. These often have a seat or statue at the end as a focal point.*

**Below:** *The trick of creating an eye-catching herbaceous border is to use plenty of contrasting shapes - upright spikes, flat-topped flowers and daisy shapes make a good basis.*

# Using spring bulbs

Spring bulbs are highly versatile flowers, and useful for bold splashes of early color all round the garden. Naturalize them permanently in borders and lawns, on banks, and as colorful carpets under trees and shrubs, or use them as temporary spring bedding plants in containers or in formal borders. Some kinds of bulbs are better for one type of use than another. Tulips are best taken out of the ground and stored 'dry' for the summer, as they rot easily if left in the ground. This makes them particularly suitable for formal uses. Dig the bulbs up after the foliage has died down naturally, rub the soil off and keep them in a cool, dark, dry place till replanting time in the fall. Daffodils, *Anemone blanda* and many other popular bulbs prefer to be left undisturbed once planted, so they are better for naturalizing. Clumps of naturalized bulbs only need to be dug up and divided when they have become so overcrowded that they no longer flower well - in this case do so when the foliage dies down after flowering, or you may have difficulty finding them. In mixed borders, plant large leafy bulbs such as daffodils towards the middle of the border, with clump-forming summer herbaceous flowers, such as hardy cranesbill, as a 'screen' in front of them - these will be growing up as the daffodil foliage is dying down. Alternatively, grow small early flowering daffodils, such as 'February Gold', that have less foliage and die down earlier.

Daffodil

Hyacinth

Crocus

Iris reticulata

Pushkinia

Anemone coronaria 'De Caen'

Ornithogalum

Allium

*Left:* Viridiflora *tulips, planted with white wallflowers against a background of interesting foliage shapes and textures, make a very attractive green and white cameo.*

Tulip

*1* *If you want to create a natural effect, the easy way to plant bulbs is to scatter them randomly over the area to be planted and then to plant them where they fall.*

*2* *In the case of large bulbs, make holes and plant to the correct depth. With small bulbs, such as anemone, which have no right way up, press them in with your finger.*

**Above:** *Anemone coronaria 'De Caen' is a favorite spring-flowering bulb that grows about 8in(20cm) tall. Plant in groups for best effect. The flowers are also good for cutting.*

Anemone blanda

Chionodoxa

Muscari

**Right:** *Most people plant bulbs far too shallowly. As a rough guide, cover the bulbs with twice their own depth of soil (measured from tip to base).*

## Ideal planting depths

Iris reticulata
2in/5cm

Crocus
3in/7.5cm

Ornithogalum
3in/7.5cm

Muscari 4in/10cm

Anemone
blanda
2in/5cm

Pushkinia
3in/7.5cm

Chionodoxa
4in/10cm

Tulip
4in/10cm

A. de Caen
2in/5cm

Allium
4in/10cm

Hyacinth
4in/10cm

Daffodil
5in/13cm

# Planting spring bulbs

Bulbs for formal planting schemes can either be planted in their proper positions in the fall, or planted in pots and plunged into place when the foliage is well grown. If the situation is well sheltered, they can even be planted when the flowers are actually coming out. This is much cheaper than buying pots of flowering bulbs in spring, and only takes a little pre-planning. However, do not take the plants out of their pots - plunge the entire pot to its rim in the soil to avoid any root damage, which would shorten the life of the flowers. Any potgrown bulbs remaining after planting spring displays and repairing gaps in borders can be brought indoors just as the flower buds start showing their true color.

**1** *Hyacinths grow well in pots. Bring them inside as they come into flower or plunge them into gaps in a border. Half fill 3.5in(9cm) pots with potting mix.*

## Planting tulips

**Left:** *Choose healthy bulbs with no traces of injury or mold, and plant them in late fall, as tulips do not start rooting until then. This prevents them rotting, which can happen if they are planted earlier. Tulips prefer being lifted and stored for the summer. This makes them ideal for areas that are to be cleared after flowering.*

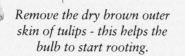

*Remove the dry brown outer skin of tulips - this helps the bulb to start rooting.*

**Above:** *A double row of tulips makes a good edging to a formal flower bed. Run two strings between canes to ensure the planting rows are straight.*

2 *Gently press a single bulb into the center of each pot. The tip should be just below the rim of the pot. Do not worry that it is not as deep as you would plant the bulb in the garden.*

3 *Fill the pot to the rim, covering the bulb completely, then tap it down gently on a hard surface to consolidate the potting mix. Add a little more mix to top up if necessary.*

4 *Water just enough to moisten the potting mix thoroughly. Allow the surplus to drain away. Put the pot in a cool place protected from excessively wet conditions, to form roots.*

*Hyacinths come about as close to true blue as you could find in spring bulbs; plant hyacinths close to a path or doorway to enjoy the full benefit of their glorious scent.*

*Plant tulips 4in(10cm) (about twice their own depth) below the soil surface.*

**Above:** *Tulips need well-drained soil to prevent them rotting, so sit the bulbs on a 1in(2.5cm) layer of coarse gritty sand in the bottom of the trench.*

**Below:** *'Queen Wilhemina' tulips growing informally in a sunny border with forget-me-nots. For best results, lift tulip bulbs when the foliage dies down. Store them in paper bags or trays in a cool, dry, dark place for the summer. Turn them occasionally and check that none of them is rotting.*

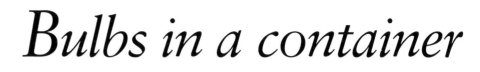

# Bulbs in a container

Containers are the ideal way of growing bulbs that need different conditions from those in the open garden; perhaps better drainage (some bulbs, such as tulips, rot easily in cold wet soil). And being portable, containers enable you to rearrange patio and doorstep displays for seasonal effect - try teaming a tub of flowering spring bulbs with all-year-round containers of evergreens or conifers. Pots of flowering bulbs are available in garden centers in spring; plunge them to the rims into tubs of old potting mix for an instant display. But it is much more satisfying to create displays with dry bulbs in fall and cheaper, too. Start with new containers and potting mixture or remove old summer bedding plants from existing containers; you can reuse the old soil, but loosen it first with a fork. Most popular spring bulbs are suitable for containers, but compact cultivars make a tighter group and are less likely to suffer broken stems in windy weather. It is best to plant each container with one type of bulb, but if you want to mix different kinds together, choose those that flower at the same time, otherwise the display will be spoiled by old foliage when the later ones come into bloom. Start liquid feeding regularly when the first buds appear.

*Soil-based potting mix*

*Gritty sand*

*1 Assemble a large clay pot, gritty sand, soil-based potting mix and your chosen bulbs. Cover the hole in the base of the pot with a broken 'crock'.*

*2 Scoop 1-2in(2.5-5cm) of gritty sand into the base of the pot to cover the crock. This provides extra drainage, which is beneficial in containers that are left out in winter.*

*3 Cover the grit with 1-2in(2.5-5cm) of potting mixture, so that the pot is roughly half-filled. Do not firm the mixture down at this stage - this is to allow bulbs to be pressed into it.*

*A soil-based potting mixture is best for bulbs, as it retains less water than peat types.*

*Use clay pots for displays of bulbs, as they are porous.*

*4 Press the bulbs gently into the potting mix. Put in as many as you can for a good display. Adjacent bulbs should not quite touch each other or the side of the pot. These are daffodils.*

*5* Cover the daffodil bulbs, leaving only the tips showing. This allows a second tier of bulbs to be planted in the gaps without risk of damage.

*6* Grape hyacinths flower at the same time as daffodils and have similar requirements, but plant them less deeply. Press the bulbs between the daffodils.

*7* Trowel more potting mix carefully over the grape hyacinth bulbs. Fill the pot to within 1in(2.5cm) of the rim. Leave some space for watering.

Lift the pot onto 'pot feet' to improve the drainage.

*8* You can stand the pot out of the way until the bulbs are in flower, but usually it is more convenient to place it in its final flowering position at this stage. Water well.

**Left:** Narcissi (daffodils) root early, so plant the bulbs as soon as they are available in late summer or early fall, especially if they are early-flowering kinds, such as 'February Gold'.

Feed bulbs well to build up their size so that they flower well again the next year.

**Right:** Grape hyacinths make delightful subjects for small pots. You can plunge the pots to their rims in windowboxes or tubs for an instant display when the bulbs are in flower.

# Bulbs under turf

One of the prettiest ways to grow spring bulbs is naturalized in grass. The most suitable types are those that are happy to be left undisturbed, such as narcissi and crocus, but many small bulbs are suitable, although hyacinths and tulips are not. Plant narcissi and crocus bulbs in natural 'drifts' (well-defined areas where bulbs are planted closely together) in an ornamental lawn to add spring interest. This creates a more colorful spectacle than dotting them about randomly, and also makes it easier to mow around growing bulbs. Rough circles of bulbs can also be naturalized under trees. Narcissi, squills (scilla), hardy cyclamen *(Cyclamen coum)*, winter aconite and snowdrops all thrive in this situation. Choose trees with light canopies or ones that are fairly late coming into leaf so that the bulbs can complete most of their growth cycle before overhead foliage cuts out the light. Bluebells and wood anemone *(Anemone nemorosa)* create a slightly wild carpet effect in light woodland. Bulbs are useful for planting on a bank, especially one that is too steep to mow safely. Here, naturalizing bulbs with wildflowers or later flowering low shrubs, such as *Hypericum*, is an effective way of covering a bank with color, suppressing weeds and avoiding the need to mow. Bulbs in grass need little attention. Apply a fall formulation lawn feed, which is low in nitrogen, over the area in early fall and again in spring. Avoid mowing over the old foliage until at least six to eight weeks after flowering.

1 *Mark out 12x36in(30x90cm) turves with a sharp spade. Slide the blade about 0.8in(2cm) below the grass to avoid severing most of the roots. Roll back turf to expose soil.*

2 *Use a fork to loosen the soil as deeply as possible. Add well-rotted and sieved organic matter, such as garden compost, if the soil is very poor, and some grit if it is very heavy.*

3 *Scatter the bulbs (these are crocus) randomly for a natural effect. Plant them where they fall using a hand trowel. Scoop out enough soil to plant each bulb at the right depth.*

4 *When all the bulbs are planted, roll the turf back into place. Firm it down lightly with the back of a rake - the whole turf must touch the soil below. Water if the weather is dry.*

*Left: Crocuses make little foliage and do not 'swamp' the grass. Delay mowing until at least six weeks after the bulb foliage has died down after flowering. Avoid using lawn feeds with weedkillers where bulbs are naturalized.*

## Using bulb planters

A bulb planter is useful for planting a few bulbs individually or for spacing them widely over a larger area. Use a bulb planter in rough or uneven grass where it is not always convenient to lift strips of turf. Still plant the bulbs at the correct depth for their type. Some bulb planters have depth markings to help - if not, use a permanent marker pen to show the required depth.

**1** Scatter bulbs, then lift each one to make a hole. Press the planter into the ground and twist to remove a core of turf and soil, which stays inside the planter.

**2** Place a single bulb in each hole. If possible, press it slightly into the soil at the base to ensure it remains upright. If the hole is too narrow and deep, simply drop the bulb down it.

**3** Re-insert the planter in the hole and squeeze the handle to drop the core of soil back into place over the bulb. Firm the soil down to level the turf with the surrounding grass.

## Planting bulbs under gravel

Bulbs such as Iris reticulata (shown here) can be naturalized on a rockery or scree garden to add spring interest to any well-drained area that is fairly dry in summer, such as graveled areas in a patio or amongst paving. Use them to create small 'cameo' features next to a garden seat or around an ornament, a large permanent container or statue.

**Below:** Dwarf iris (Iris reticulata) flowers in early spring. These bulbs need good drainage; grow them in a rockery or raised bed and lay 1-2in (2.5-5cm) of gravel over the area after planting.

**1** Excavate a shallow depression with a trowel where the bulbs are to go. This should be the correct planting depth for the type of bulbs used. Add grit if the soil needs extra drainage. Scatter the bulbs randomly.

**2** Press the bulbs gently into place and twist slightly to ensure good contact with the soil. Cover with soil, making sure bulbs remain upright.

**3** When the soil is level with the surrounding area, add a thin layer of stone chippings as a mulch. This also makes a decorative finish.

# Planning a spring border

After a long dull winter, the first spring flowers are always welcome, but instead of just dotting them around the garden, make them into more of a spectacle by concentrating them together in a spring border. This does not have to be an isolated feature that looks dull for the rest of the year - spring plants can be happily integrated into a summer border, where they provide the starting point for a long season of color. Plan the border so that there is a good balance between spring and summer flowers - the foliage of spring flowers will provide a leafy 'foil' for those that follow on later. Plant tall summer flowers, such as delphiniums, towards the back of the border; spring kinds tend to be low-growing, so plant them towards the front. Low bulbs, such as *Anemone blanda*, make a colorful carpet under shrubs and towards the front of the border, while taller kinds, such as daffodils, are best kept in clumps towards the middle, where the untidy foliage will be partly hidden by other plants. Buy pots of spring annuals, such as polyanthus, colored primroses and forget-me-not, already in flower, to fill any odd gaps. In a large garden where there is room, you could create a spring 'cameo' purely from early flowers, which makes a much more solid effect. It also gives you a chance to create interesting plant associations based around favorite plants, such as euphorbias, *Epimedium* and hellebores. For a specially striking yellow trio, try *Euphorbia wulfenii*, narcissi and the early yellow *Paeonia mlokosewitschii*.

**Above:** *Forget-me-nots, with bluebells, tulips,* Helleborus orientalis *and* Dicentra spectabilis *'Alba'.*

Cheiranthus 'Bowles Mauve'

Dicentra formosa

Doronicum orientale (leopard's bane)

Dicentra spectabilis 'Alba'

Bergenia 'Ballawley'

Primula denticulata

Primula rosea 'Grandiflora'

**Above:** *Daffodils and* Helleborus foetidus *(stinking hellebore) make a successful plant association. Despite its name, the hellebore does not smell unpleasant unless leaves are damaged.*

**Above:** Paeonia mlokosewitschii *is a beautiful early-flowering species, which for obvious reasons is better known by its common name of 'Mollie the Witch'.*

**Above:** Euphorbia wulfenii *has striking lime green spring flowers. This is a canary yellow form of it called 'Lambrook's Gold', which must be propagated from cuttings.*

Narcissus 'Hawera'

Primula vulgaris flore-plena 'Dawn Ansell'

Hyacinths

Ranunculus (turban buttercup)

Primula vulgaris (cultivated primrose)

Pansies

Primula rosea

Tulip 'Orange Nassau'

Viola 'Prince Henry'

# Planting up a hanging basket

Summer would not be summer without hanging baskets. Suspended from brackets, they are the ideal way to decorate a doorway or a stretch of wall, and they can hang from the ends of pergola poles or special free-standing basket supports anywhere in the garden. Hanging baskets are traditionally used to create spectacular displays by blending together a mixture of upright, trailing and chunkier-shaped annual bedding plants in a wide range of colors. However, there are many variations. You could plant a large group of identical plants in the same basket to give the effect of a huge ball of blooms. Try five trailing fuchsias of the same variety in the top of the basket, or plant compact bedding plants, such as impatiens, in the top and through the sides of an open lattice-sided basket. You can design hanging gardens that complement nearby tubs by using similar plants or a matching color scheme. Another new idea is to plant very long dangly and tough foliage houseplants with trailing annuals, such as lobelia, in baskets for the summer; use *Saxifraga sarmentosa* 'Tricolor', Swedish ivy *(Plectranthus)*, ivies or spider plant *(Chlorophytum)* - by fall they trail down almost to ground level. And why not plant things that twine upwards? Black-eyed Susan, canary creeper *(Tropaeolum peregrinum)* and morning glories will drape themselves round the outside of a basket and cover the chains, brackets and nearby trellis with their huge colorful flowers.

*1 Stand an open-weave wire basket on a bucket for stability and then line it - this is green-dyed natural coconut fiber.*

*2 The lining should be thick enough to retain the soil. Fill the center of the basket with soilless potting mixture.*

*3 Assemble your plants; these are dwarf pelargonium, trailing lobelia, French marigolds, coleus and the lime green form of Helichrysum petiolatum.*

*4 Plant the tallest flower in the middle of the basket; this will add height to the arrangement. As you plant, remove any yellow leaves or spent flowerheads.*

**5** One side of the basket will form the front of the display, so plant a pair of flowers, one on either side of the central plant, for a symmetrical arrangement.

**6** Tuck in the coleus; choose plants with complementary colors. Coleus are grown for their foliage; nip out flower buds or leaves lose their color.

Pack plants in closely together for a fuller display.

**7** Fill in any odd gaps with lobelia, which will cascade down over the sides of the basket. The Helichrysum, planted at the back of the basket, will create a leafy, lime backdrop.

**8** Water well in after planting. Traditional baskets dry out very quickly, so check at least daily and water before the soil gets bone dry.

Coleus are available in a wide range of foliage colors and make a welcome addition to hanging baskets and other potted summer arrangements.

**9** Hang the completed basket in a spot where it will receive direct sun for at least half the day, but is sheltered from drying winds. Remove dead flowerheads regularly to keep the basket looking at its best all summer.

**1** *The secret of success when pairing plants and containers is to put everything together in a group before buying, so you can gauge the effect.*

# Planting up a plastic cauldron

One of the things that makes container gardening fun is the way you can keep finding new combinations of pots and plants that work well together. Try out new kinds of plants that you find in garden centers and do not always go for the same species, color schemes or style. And experiment with different kinds of containers - even ones that perhaps look a little unlikely to start with. There is no need to spend a fortune. Cheap plastic containers can be made to look sensational, given the right sort of plants to bring out their hidden depths, and secondhand 'finds' in junk shops or rummage sales can be given a new lease of life with an unusual paint effect or simply by cleaning them up. If you cannot take an existing container to the nursery with you, try to find something similar in the shop and stand your basket of plants next to it to see how they look. Also look at the striking ready-planted containers that many garden centers set up, both to tempt people who prefer not to bother making up their own, but to give good ideas to those who do. If you grow your own plants from seed, you can judge the effect of various flowers and containers by cutting pictures from magazines and catalogs - that way, you can have all the fun of planning your summer displays in midwinter, in good time to send off your seed order.

**2** *Almost fill the container to the rim with potting mixture and knock each plant in turn out of its pot. Avoid breaking the rootball.*

**3** *Position the largest and most striking plant in the center of the container and fit the others around its roots in the remaining space.*

**6** *Use the shortest plants at the front of the display, encouraging them where possible to spill over the front of the container, thus softening the hard line of the edge.*

Pelargonium

Striped single
French marigolds

*Calceolaria (new colorful outdoor strains, resembling those previously only available as indoor pot plants).*

French
marigolds

**4** Group plants with different shaped flowers next to each other. Plant the palest species towards the front to add depth to the display.

**5** Use a narrow trowel to tuck spare soil into the gaps between rootballs. When all the plants are in place, add 0.5in(1.25cm) of soil over the entire surface.

French
marigolds

Mini outdoor
'Carnival'
chrysanthemums

Mimulus

# Summer-flowering bulbs

If you mention bulbs, most people think of spring-flowering daffodils and tulips, but there are plenty of less well-known kinds that flower in summer. Some, such as gladioli, acidanthera, *Eucomis* (pineapple flower), tuberous begonia and tigridia, are not hardy enough to leave in the ground through the winter, so plant them in spring. In the fall, when the flowers are over and the foliage dies down, dig them up, dry them off and store them in a frost-free place. Summer-flowering bulbs that can be planted permanently in a mild climate include summer hyacinths *(Galtonia)*, which have large sprays of greenish white flowers similar to those of yucca, and *Crinum powellii*, the giant of the summer bulbs. Each one has a long thick neck that must remain above ground when it is planted. Give it rich soil. A hot, sunny, flower bed at the foot of a wall is the best place to grow nerine and *Amaryllis hippeastrum* (not to be confused with the indoor plant *Hippeastrum*). Both like to be planted and then left undisturbed, without other plants around them to prevent the bulbs ripening properly. The flowers appear in late summer or fall on bare stems, after the leaves have died down. All summer bulbs need a sunny sheltered spot and well-drained soil to thrive. Prepare the soil well before planting, by forking in a handful of general fertilizer per square yard, and plenty of well-rotted organic matter - coir is ideal for summer bulbs, as it improves the soil structure without holding too much moisture. Summer bulbs are not always readily available in garden centers - in case of difficulty, buy mail order from a specialist bulb catalog.

**1** *To plant a canna, choose a pot large enough to take the roots with ease. Part fill it with potting mix and rest the tuber on the surface, allowing for 2in(5cm) of mix above the tip.*

Galtonia candicans
*(summer hyacinth)*

*Large-flowered gladiolus*

Canna *'Lucifer'*

Eucomis bicolor

Acidanthera murielae

Tigridia pavonia

*Miniature* Gladiolus orchidiolus

**2** Cover the tuber with more potting mix and then fill the pot almost to the rim. Tap the pot down firmly to consolidate the potting mixture.

**3** Leave a 1in(2.5cm) gap between the surface of the potting mix and the rim of the pot for watering. Water until the soil is evenly wet; allow any surplus to drain away.

**4** Keep the pot in a slightly heated greenhouse or sunroom or on a sunny windowsill until there is no danger of frost. Then you can safely put it outdoors.

*Repot as necessary. An established canna makes a large plant that needs a 10in(25cm)-pot or even more.*

## Ideal planting depths

Acidanthera *(6in/15cm)*

Galtonia *(6in/15cm,*

*Large-flowered* Gladiolus *(4in/10cm)*

Eucomis *(4in/10cm)*

Miniature Gladiolus *(3in/7.5cm)*

Canna *(2in/5cm)*

Tigridia *(2in/5cm)*

**Right:** *A canna planted in a pot will not grow as tall as it would in a border. Expect flowers in mid- to late summer. If kept well fed, the tuber will be larger the following year and may produce more than one flower spike.*

## Canna in a pot

If you grow summer-flowering bulbs in pots in a frost-free place, they will start to flower earlier than dormant bulbs planted straight into the garden soil. Canna is a particularly good plant to grow in this way, as it makes a good summer pot plant for the patio; you can also plunge the pot to the rim in a bed of annuals as a 'dot' plant.

# The magnificent lilies

Lilies are one of the most spectacular and collectable summer-flowering bulbs. Some varieties need lime-free soil, while others do not mind. Most prefer to be grown in a border surrounded by other plants, with the bulbs shaded but their tops in sun, while others enjoy shady woodland conditions. Some lilies are good for growing in pots on a patio, but if your soil is not suitable for the species you want to grow, any lilies can be grown in large pots containing a suitable potting mixture, sunk into the ground. Full cultural details of individual varieties can be found in the catalog (if bought by mail order) or on the back of the pack (if you buy at a garden center). Although pot-grown plants are available in flower during the summer, lilies are normally bought as dry bulbs in spring. Regardless of other requirements, all lilies need good-quality, well-drained, moisture-retentive soil when grown in the garden. Add plenty of well rotted organic matter (coir is ideal) and gritty sand before planting. As an extra precaution against rotting, place a generous layer of gritty sand at the base of each planting hole. Plant the Madonna lily *(Lilium candidum)* with the tip of the bulb just showing above ground, but as a general rule, plant lily bulbs so that they are covered by twice their own depth of soil. Plant three or five lilies of the same variety together in a group, spaced 4-6in(10-15cm) apart, for a good show. Once planted, lilies need not be dug up or divided until groups are overcrowded and lack vigor. Mulch generously each spring and feed regularly during the growing season as they are heavy feeders.

*Choose good-quality bulbs.*

*1 Assemble six bulbs, soil-based potting mix and a 14in(15.5cm) diameter pot (to allow sufficient planting depth). Half-fill the pot.*

*2 Place the lilies on the potting mix, spaced an equal distance apart. In pots, you can plant lilies closer together than you would in a garden.*

*3 Arrange five bulbs around the edge of the pot and one in the center. Cover the bulbs with potting mix; make sure that they stay upright.*

*4 Once it is in flower, you can stand a pot-grown lily on a patio (but make sure that the pot is in shade) or sink the pot to its rim in a border for instant color in a vacant spot.*

**Below:** *As a general rule, plant lily bulbs so that the tip of each bulb is covered by 6in(15cm) of soil. The soil should be moisture-retentive but well-drained, and not too wet in winter.*

**Above:** *To plant lilies outdoors, lay the bulbs informally on the prepared soil, about 12in(30cm) apart. Dig individual holes for each bulb.*

**Below:** *Here lilies are planted with a cut-leaved elder and lady's mantle. Try planting them with a low foreground of shorter plants to keep bulbs cool.*

**Left:** *Lilies flower in summer; since their blooms are large and exotic-looking, a good leafy background shows them off to advantage. This variety is 'Journey's End'. Plant groups of different varieties for a long succession of lily flowers throughout the summer months.*

# Connoisseur's flowers – something special

Given a few years growing experience, it is not unnatural to develop a particular interest in one group of plants, and to hunt out unusual, new, old or rare cultivars. Before you know it, you have started a collection. People collect all kinds of plants - hostas, old-fashioned roses, alpines, and rare hardy plants generally. Several specialist societies exist to help enthusiasts obtain and learn about choice plants. (For details of membership consult gardening magazines.) Collectables often have unique 'personalities' or cultivation requirements, and their foibles are all part of the attraction to a collector. Old roses for instance have very distinctive flowers, blowsy and often 'quartered', with a range of colors and scents often lacking in modern kinds. However, they suffer from one drawback to general gardeners, namely a very short flowering season, only six to eight weeks in early summer. One breeder of modern roses has got round this by producing New English Roses, which have the distinctive flowers of old roses combined with the long flowering season of modern kinds. These are just as easy to grow as normal roses. Some collectable plants, however, need special attention.

The reason scarce plants are in short supply is usually because they are difficult to propagate, or need very precise growing conditions and cultivation. Choice alpines, for example, are often grown in pots and protected in winter in specially constructed greenhouses or cold frames. Whole beds may be designed around a collection of one particular alpine species.

*Left: Gold-laced polyanthus were 'florists flowers', bred and exhibited by 18th century flower fanciers in the UK. Once, hundreds of named varieties existed. Now only this and the silver-laced polyanthus remain, but they are still very lovely.*

*Above: Auriculas were also old 'florists flowers', although today they are again very collectable and plenty of new varieties are being bred. 'Argus' shown here was raised in 1895. Modern varieties are easier to come by and simpler to cultivate.*

**Right:** Rosa Mundi (Rosa gallica versicolor) *is said to date back to the 12th century, when it was named after Henry II's mistress, the fair Rosamunde. It grows to 48x48in (120x120cm). It is easy to grow and stays fairly disease-free.*

**Right:** Rosa chinensis mutabilis *is one of the China roses; this one has pink- or purple-tinged young foliage. Species roses of all kinds are gaining in popularity today. As they often make large prickly plants, they are good for hedging or wild gardens.*

**Left:** *'Graham Thomas' is one of the best New English Roses, named after one of the most influential rose experts. The plant grows to 48x48in (120x120cm) and has tea-scented flowers all summer.*

53

# Charming sweet peas

*Left: Sweet peas can make a striking feature, as here in a terracotta pot, with plants trained to climb up a rustic wigwam of loosely interwoven willow wands.*

Sweet peas are surprisingly versatile traditional favorites. They are good both as cut flowers and garden plants. Grow them up a 'tent' of twiggy pea sticks to give height to a border, or as climbers on trellis or netting. Knee-high dwarf cultivars can be grown in hanging baskets, and as low-flowering summer 'hedges', edging lawns or borders. Any sweet peas can be cut for indoors - the more you cut, the more flowers are produced. However, sweet peas that have been allowed to ramble freely often have short, kinked or bent stems. If you want sweet peas with long straight stems for cutting, grow them as cordons. Here, each plant is trained individually up a cane as a single stem, secured with plant rings or raffia. Nip out the thin curly tendrils between thumb and finger, otherwise they 'grab' hold of the flower stems, making them kink. Seed catalogs list a huge range of different named varieties of sweet peas and mixtures are also available. Not all varieties are well perfumed, so check the descriptions. Old-fashioned cultivars, such as 'Painted Lady' and the various old-fashioned mixtures that are sometimes available, are best in this respect. Their flowers are not as large as in the modern, wavy-edged, Spencer types, but their scent makes up for it. Even if you do not cut sweet peas for the house, remove deadheads at least once a week, otherwise the plants quickly stop flowering.

**1** *Sow sweet pea seeds spaced 1.5in (3.75cm) square in a tray filled with seed sowing mixture. You can sow the seeds in early fall for early flowers, but spring is the usual time for sowing them.*

**2** *Push each seed into the sowing mixture until it just disappears below the surface. The seeds should be buried to their own depth in the sowing mixture.*

**3** Pinch the sowing mix together over the top of each seed to fill the hole. If necessary, sprinkle a fine layer of extra sowing mix over the surface.

**4** Water thoroughly and let surplus moisture drain away. Large seeds absorb a great deal of water before germinating so check the soil regularly.

**5** Cover with a plastic propagator lid to help maintain humidity during germination. When the first shoots appear, slide back the vents.

*Above:* A flowering sweet pea hedge, produced by spacing plants about 12in(30cm) apart and training them up a post and netting fence. Regular cutting encourages new buds.

*Left:* Sweet peas hold themselves up to trellis or netting using their tendrils, but these also tangle together and catch on neighboring flower stems, making them bend or kink.

**6** Remove the lid entirely when the shoots are 1in(2.5cm) high. Gradually acclimatize the plants to harder conditions by standing them outside when the weather is fine.

*You can easily remove the growing tip by nipping it out between thumb and forefinger.*

**7** When the seedlings have two true leaves, nip out the growing tip of the plant to encourage branching. The sideshoots that develop can also be 'stopped' after two leaves for nice bushy plants.

# Tuberous begonias in tubs

Tuberous begonias are very useful flowers all around the house and garden. Use them on windowsills, in sunrooms, porches or a greenhouse, and outdoors in containers or beds. There are various types: the normal, upright-growing, double-flowered plant in a range of colors; trailing begonias for hanging baskets; and cultivars with unusual flower forms, such as anemone-centered, semi-double or frilled-edged. The very large-flowered kinds are intended for exhibition and need greenhouse cultivation. In spring, you can buy dry, dormant begonia tubers, which are easy to grow. Established plants in pots are also available all summer. However, the cheapest way to acquire a good collection is to grow your own from seed. Sprinkle the dustlike seed thinly on the surface of finely sifted seed mixture, and cover the pot with plastic film. Stand the pot in a dish of tepid water until it is completely moist. Keep it in a warm place at a steady temperature and out of direct sunlight. When the seedlings are large enough, prick them out individually into a tray of similar seed mix, and cover them with a plastic propagator lid to retain humidity. Finally, pot the seedlings individually into small pots. Expect seed-raised plants to start flowering in their second year.

Tuberous begonias lose their stems and leaves in the fall; when they start yellowing in late summer, reduce the feed and water until the soil in the pots is quite dry. Store the pots in a dry, frost-free place for the winter, or empty the pots and store the dry tubers in paper bags in a drawer indoors.

*Above:* To produce large blooms on a tuberous begonia, nip out the two tiny buds on either side of the main flower. This variety is called 'Pin Up'.

**1** *To avoid planting begonia tubers upside down, sit the dry corms convex side up in a dish of damp seed mixture on a warm windowsill.*

**2** *When fat pink buds are visible in the dished surface of the corm, you can be certain it has started to grow and is the right way up, although no roots have appeared yet. This is the right stage for potting.*

**3** *To plant the corm, loosely fill a 4 or 5in(10 or 13cm) diameter pot with potting mixture to within 0.5in(1.25cm) of the rim. The potting mixture can be either peat, coir or soil-based.*

**Left:** *A row of similar tuberous begonias makes an attractive semi-formal feature in a terracotta trough. The effect is of a cottage windowsill. Deadhead regularly to keep new buds coming all summer.*

**Right:** *Trailing tuberous begonias are good for hanging baskets, here seen growing with fuchsia, lobelia, busy lizzie and petunias. Trailing begonias need not be disbudded, as they naturally have many smaller flowers.*

**5** *The end result: a well-grown begonia plant with perfect blooms the size of tea cups that make a stunning display in their container.*

**Right:** *Once the plant is coming into flower, you can transfer it to a larger container, such as this formal outdoor urn.*

**4** *Press the base of the corm firmly into the center of the pot, leaving the very top of the corm just showing above the surface. Water; keep out of bright sun until growing well.*

# Late season border

Towards the end of the season, many herbaceous borders are looking past their best as summer flowers come to an end. But there are plenty of species that flower in late summer. By planting these among the summer-flowering kinds, the late bloomers provide foliage that acts as a foil to summer flowers, then take over the interest from them as the earlier flowers are deadheaded or cut down. (Some early summer flowers, such as delphiniums and lupins, give a second, later show if they are cut down almost to ground level as soon as the flowers are finished). To make the most of late flowers, plant tall kinds behind shorter summer flowers and make sure that all plants are given sufficiently wide spacing, otherwise it is easy to find your late crop of flowers have been smothered by earlier plants. Short late flowers, such as *Liriope muscari,* and clumps of fall bulbs, such as colchicums, are useful for planting at the front of the border to mask seasonal gaps. To make the most of a late display, do not allow your vigilance to slip in midsummer, when a border of summer flowers could safely be allowed to 'slip' a little. Make sure that you regularly deadhead the whole border and cut down early flowers to ground level when the foliage starts dying down, so that late flowers stand out against clean foliage. For much the same reasons, it is important not to get behind with routine chores, including weeding, feeding and slug control, if you want a good late show from your border. And have a few pots of late-sown annuals (sown thinly in pots in early summer and planted out in a clump) ready to tuck into any bare gaps for an instant show of color.

*Left: Purples, mauves, oranges and yellows are the colors that dominate a late border. Here, they are provided by Sedum spectabile, Rudbeckia, Solidago (golden rod) and Michaelmas daisies.*

**Left:** Diascia flanaganii *flowers from midsummer well into the fall. The plants make spreading carpets about 6-9in(15-23cm) high that look good contrasting with silver artemisias.*

**Right:** Rudbeckia 'Goldsturm' *and* Salvia farinacea *both flower well through late summer and the fall, until the first serious frosts cut them back.*

## Late summer flowers

Aconitum autumnale
Agapanthus *(African lily)*
Anemone japonica
Aster amellus, ericoides, novae angliae *(New England asters)*
Aster novi-belgii *(Michaelmas daisies)*, Cimicifuga *(bugbane)*
Dendranthema *(formerly* Chrysanthemum) rubellum *(hardy cottage chrysanthemums)*
Helianthus *(perennial sunflower)*
Heliopsis
Kniphofia 'Little Maid' *and* 'Percy's Pride', Ligularia
Liriope muscari, Penstemon
Phlox, Physalis franchetii
Phygelius, Rudbeckia fulgida
Schizostylis *(kaffir lily)*
Solidago *(golden rod)*
Tricyrtis *(toad lily)*

## Keeping summer annuals in flower

*Many summer annuals can be kept flowering till fall. Keep them regularly fed, never let them go short of water and nip off all the dying flowerheads as soon as you spot them. Check plants over at least once a week.*

**Right:** *There are several named varieties of the butterfly plant,* Sedum spectabile. *All make good late-flowering plants, with the added bonus of striking foliage decorated with heads of vivid green buds earlier in the summer. Good for cutting.*

# Dazzling dahlias

1 Choose a pot large enough to take the dahlia tuber with room to spare and half fill it with potting mixture. Sit the tuber in the middle.

2 Cover the tuber with 2in(5cm) of potting mix, filling the pot almost to the rim. Tap the pot down sharply to consolidate the potting mix.

3 Water and put in a frost-free place. When the first shoots are 3-4in(7.5-10cm) tall, you can remove a few to use as cuttings if you wish.

After a long spell out of fashion, dahlias are back in favor again. They make superb free-flowering plants for midsummer to fall displays, but their large, distinctive flowers can easily overpower more delicate neighbors, so they need placing with care. Plant them in groups among spring and early summer-flowering shrubs to brighten up the border later in the year or keep them to a bed of their own. Dahlia flowers are wonderful for cutting, and the more you pick, the more you get. Named varieties are available with flowers ranging from tiny to gigantic, and from neat pompon shapes to open-faced collarettes and spiky-petaled cactus types, in virtually every color except true blue. Dahlias are grown from tubers planted out in late spring, about two weeks before the last frost. A small selection is available in garden centers as dry tubers in spring, but enthusiasts send for catalogs from specialist nurseries or order plants at flower shows in late summer. Rooted cuttings are occasionally available in spring, but do not plant these out until after the last frost. Dahlias need moist, rich soil in a sunny spot and some regular attention for best results. Plants continue flowering right up to the first fall frosts. In mild areas with free-draining soil, some people can get away with leaving dahlia tubers in the ground over the winter, protecting the tubers under a deep layer of leaf litter. Elsewhere, lift and store them (see panel).

*Right:* Compact dahlias make good plants for the front of a border, but they are also good grown in pots - try them on a patio, or plunged to their rims to fill late gaps in borders.

## Lifting and storing dahlia tubers

*Leave plants in the ground until early frosts start to blacken the foliage. Cut the stems down to 6in(15cm) and dig the plants up carefully to avoid damaging the tubers. Turn them upside down so that the sap can drain out of the hollow stems. When they are completely dry, rub any soil off the tubers. Store them in a dry, frost-free shed, away from rodents. Check the tubers regularly, and if you see any rot, cut out the affected area and dust the cut surface with yellow or green horticultural sulfur.*

*Cut dahlias when there are plenty of tight petals in the center of the bloom for longest vase life. Stand them in deep tepid water.*

*Cactus-flowered dahlias are characterized by quilted petals.*

**1** To grow dahlias in a border, dig a hole into well-prepared soil, about 8in(20cm) deep and wide enough to take the tuber with space to spare.

**2** Place the tuber on top of a small mound of soil in the bottom of the hole, and space the roots out so that they make good contact with the soil.

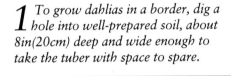

**Above:** The tip of the tuber should be 6in(15cm) below the ground. If a late frost threatens the first shoots, cover them with bracken or peat.

**Right:** Dahlias make good cut flowers. Shake them lightly to dislodge any earwigs and put the stems into water immediately after cutting them.

**3** Hammer in a strong stake just behind the tuber. If you leave this till later you risk damaging the tuber. Cover the tuber and fill the hole.

*Remove lower leaves before arranging or they make the water slimy.*

*Top up the water in vases daily, as dahlias are heavy drinkers.*

61

# Winter and spring displays

The best plants for winter color are 'Universal' pansies and cultivated primrose hybrids. These will flower reliably throughout winter given a sheltered sunny situation in a reasonably mild climate. Elsewhere they will flower on and off during mild spells. Ornamental cabbages are another excellent choice. Garden centers and nurseries now sell spring bulbs, polyanthus, wallflowers, etc., in pots, already in flower and ready to plant out for an instant display. Use winter and spring bedding to create a complete bed in a sheltered sunny spot close to the house, where it can be seen easily. Or use well-chosen groups of plants to liven up shrub borders, or fill seasonal gaps in a perennial bed. Prepare the soil well before planting winter and spring bedding. Fork it over, removing weeds, roots and debris. Fertilizer should not be necessary if the soil is fertile and has been well cultivated, but a sprinkling of bonemeal can be beneficial. Rake the soil level, then plant. Space winter flowers close together to make a dense carpet of color that shows up well from a distance.

**2** Add primroses, already coming into flower, all round the cabbage. Tip each plant carefully out of its pot and plant it without disturbing the roots or breaking the developing buds.

**1** Begin by planting a frieze of wallflowers at the back of the border. Next add the largest, most striking plant - here an ornamental cabbage - which will form the centerpiece of the display.

**3** *Plant primroses so that they are almost touching - they will not grow any bigger now. This way they will form a solid carpet of color when fully out in flower. Mix the colors well.*

*Wallflower. Plants bought in spring look less weather beaten than those that have been out in the open all winter.*

**4** *Water the plants in well after planting. Give them a weak liquid feed during mild spells and remove dead flowerheads and yellow leaves regularly to keep plants flowering.*

*Ornamental cabbages are as good as flowers and equally reliable, but expect them to run to seed in late winter.*

### For *winter and early spring bedding*

*Universal pansies
Bellis daisies
Forget me not
Spring bulbs*

*Perennial plants to put with them temporarily*

*Euonymus
Dwarf conifers
Winter-flowering heathers*

**Left:** *Wallflowers (Cheiranthus 'Fire King') and tulips (Tulipa 'West Point') combine attractively to create a colorful late spring display.*

*Cultivated primrose hybrids (Primula acaulis hybrids)*

# A winter hanging basket

Given a reasonably sheltered sunny spot, it is possible to keep hanging baskets looking good all winter. Choose from the limited range of suitable flowers backed up by plenty of evergreens. The most reliable winter flowers are 'Universal' pansies and hybrid primroses. (Other winter-flowering pansies are available, but the more expensive 'Universal' strain flowers even in cold weather; hybrid primroses are like colored versions of the wild kind, and with bigger flowers - they start flowering much earlier than the rather similar polyanthus.) Add small evergreens such as ivy, euonymus, santolina or periwinkle (variegated versions are specially pretty). Use the trailing kinds around the edge for a fuller, softer effect. In big cities, the microclimate often makes it possible to grow relatively tender plants outdoors in winter; almost hardy indoor plants such as cyclamen, winter cherry, cineraria and asparagus fern often thrive. Look around the neighborhood, and if other people can grow them, go ahead. There is no need to buy special hanging baskets for winter displays; you can reuse ordinary summer ones, but avoid those with built-in drip trays or water reservoirs unless the basket is to be kept under cover - excess watering can be a problem in winter.

*1 Assemble the plants, basket and potting mixture. If it has a rounded base, sit the basket in an upturned bucket to make it easier to work on. Drape the chains over the outside.*

*Choose variegated or frilly green kinds of ivy to contrast with the flowers.*

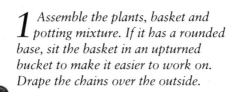

*2 Three-quarters fill the basket with potting mixture. This leaves room for the rootballs of your plants, which will virtually fill the top 3in (7.5cm) of space in the basket. Remove plants from their pots before planting.*

*3 Put in the plants without disturbing the rootballs. (This ensures that the flowers and buds do not receive a check in growth that could abort them.) Tuck them close together.*

**4** Add trailing ivies around the edges; they will partly cover the sides of the basket and create a fuller, more rounded display.

Cultivated primrose hybrids (Primula acaulis *hybrids*)

Winter-flowering pansies

Variegated ivy

Plants in hanging baskets must be able to withstand exposure to severe weather.

**5** When all the plants have been put in, trickle some potting mixture between the rootballs so that no roots are left exposed to the air, then water thoroughly. Add more soil if some has been washed down into the basket.

**6** Hang the basket in a sunny sheltered spot - a porch or under a car port is ideal, otherwise on a wall that receives the sun. Check to see if it needs watering every week, and apply a weak liquid feed in mild weather.

# Winter-flowering tubs

All the plants suggested for winter hanging baskets are equally suitable for containers. Being closer to ground level, tubs suffer less from the weather, so you can grow a wider range of plants, including winter-flowering heathers (page 69), Christmas rose *(Helleborus niger)*, early spring bulbs and any of the early spring bedding plants (page 62). It is also possible to use taller plants, such as evergreen shrubs, as the centerpiece of a floral display; variegated or colored kinds, such as euonymus and *Choisya ternata* 'Sundance', whipcord *Hebe* 'James Stirling' or dwarf conifers, are good. Plants bought straight from a garden center are ideal. Shrubs can remain in their new containers for a couple of years, but will fairly quickly fill them with root, preventing new bedding plants being put in to replace those that are over. So unless the plant is to become a solo specimen, repot it with new flowers into a larger container each fall, or plant it out into the garden in spring. Stand winter tubs in a reasonably sheltered sunny spot, ideally in front of a wall for extra protection, and raise the base of the container up on 'pot feet' or bricks so that excess water can drain away.

## Container plants

*Choose only the best plants for containers as they are always 'on show'. Reject any without plenty of buds or any with unhealthy leaves. Anticipate problems if the soil is bone dry or plants appear neglected. Well cared for plants in bud with a few flowers just open and fresh green foliage are best buys. Before planting remove any dead flowers or yellow leaves.*

**3** *First, put the largest plant in the center of the tub. Keep the rootball intact, as space will be short and there are several other plants to put in.*

**2** *With a crock covering the hole in the base of the pot to prevent soil from running out, fill the tub to within a few inches of its rim with any good soil-based potting mix.*

**1** *Gather together a large container, potting mix and a variety of plants. For a colorful formal display, choose a compact evergreen shrub, trailing ivies and winter-flowering annuals.*

Young, pot-grown
winter-flowering
evergreens, such as
Skimmia japonica
'Rubella', look good
in containers

Variegated ivy

Cultivated primrose
hybrids (Primula
acaulis hybrids)

**4** A large plant, such as ivy, trailing over the tub, softens the straight edges and helps the evergreen to blend in with the arrangement.

**5** Tuck flowering plants around the edge of the pot. Their colors should blend with the buds on the shrub.

**6** Fit in as many flowering plants as possible. Once in bloom, they do not grow any more, so the finished result must provide the full impact.

**7** Pull out strands of ivy for a wispy effect. Sit the arrangement in a prominent position. Water in well. Apply a weak feed during mild spells.

# Perennial flowers in tubs

A perennial planting scheme is an attractive low-maintenance alternative for busy gardeners. This way you plant once, then carry out routine maintenance for two to three years. At the end of this time, the plants will need splitting up and replanting into fresh potting mixture. Because perennial flowers do not have the same long flowering season as bedding plants, the best plan is to have several sets of tubs permanently planted with flowers for spring, summer, fall and winter color. By including at least one good foliage plant in each scheme, the containers will always offer something of interest even when not in flower. They make good backgrounds for other containers that are flowering - just switch them round so the 'best' one is on show. All sorts of perennials make good container plants. Choose compact kinds that flower over a long period for best effect. As long as they all need similar conditions, you can mix several small or slow-growing kinds together in the same container. For a really striking display, use several matching containers of different sizes, some planted with a mixture of plants and others with individual large specimens.

*2 Partly fill the container with potting mixture. Choose a flame-shaped dwarf conifer for the centerpiece, remove it from its pot and plant it in the middle without breaking up the rootball.*

*This wide, shallow terracotta 'dish' suits a heather mixture very nicely.*

*1 Assemble the plants and select an appropriately sized container for them. Cover the hole in the base with a curved crock for good drainage.*

**3** Remove each heather in turn from its pot. Squeeze the rootball slightly to flatten it so that it fits the space, and drop it into place around the conifer. Tuck more soil around and under it.

**4** Plant the rest of the heathers, tucking them closely together to create a complete carpet of foliage under the conifer.

## Perennials for tubs

*Choose winter-flowering heathers for a winter display. All the ones used here are cultivars of Calluna vulgaris, Erica x darleyensis and Erica carnea. Tubs are useful for restricting plants that naturally spread excessively; variegated ground elder, Houttuynia 'Chameleon' and eau-de-cologne mint are superb in tubs. Large, clump-forming plants, such as Agapanthus and ornamental grasses, often look more effective in a container of their own and cannot swamp their neighbors.*

**5** As you add the remaining heathers, alternate flowering plants with those in tight bud for a balanced display. Water the plants well in, then stand the completed container on 'pot feet' to raise the base above ground level and improve drainage. This is vital for a successful winter display. Choose a sunny sheltered spot.

Chamaecyparis lawsoniana 'Ellwoods Gold'

Mixed winter-flowering heathers

69

# Cottage garden borders

Nowadays, many people with modern houses have a cottage garden. The popular 'recipe' includes roses round the door, hollyhocks at the gate, flowers mixed with vegetables, fruit trees instead of flowering shrubs, and no lawn but gravel paths edged with flowers or low lavender hedges everywhere. However, most people today want at least a small lawn, and vegetables grown amongst flowers are never as productive as when grown in rows in a proper vegetable garden. The real secret of a successful cottage garden is to have carpets of plants covering the borders so that no soil is visible, and to grow plants that look 'cottagey' even if they are not entirely authentic. Old-fashioned annuals, such as godetia, wallflowers, snapdragons, clarkia and alyssum, can be allowed to seed themselves about randomly - simply pull up any that grow where they are not wanted. Rampant spreading plants like golden rod, lemon balm *(Melissa officinalis)* and many of the herbaceous campanulas can be grouped in a bed of their own and left to fight for space. These are useful for creating a low-maintenance cottage garden, although the result can be a little on the wild side for many people's liking.

**Above:** *A plain picket fence and old-fashioned flowers such as these snapdragons create an unsophisticated feeling of 'olde worlde' charm.*

**Left:** *When you mention cottage gardens, this is what immediately springs to mind: riotous borders overflowing with a huge mixture of flowers apparently fighting for space.*

## Other cottage styles

*As an alternative, try beds of roses underplanted with low carpeting herbaceous flowers, with tall delphiniums, tree mallow and thalictrum growing through towards the back. Enthusiasts also find room for choice cottage 'treasures', such as gold-laced polyanthus, old-fashioned pinks and auriculas, which need special care to thrive.*

*Right: Many wildflowers are old cottage garden plants. Obtain seeds from specialist suppliers; do not take plants or seeds from the wild.*

## Popular plants for cottage gardens

Astrantia
Aquilegia
*Crown imperials*
*Cultivated primroses*
*Daffodils*
*Forget-me-not*
*Hardy fuchsia*
*Honeysuckle*
*Lavender*
*Myrtle*
*Nasturtium*
*Pinks*
Pulmonaria
Pyrethrum
*Rosemary*
*Old-fashioned roses*
Sedum acre *(stonecrop)*
Sempervivum arachnoideum
*(cobwebbed houseleek)*
*Sweet william, Wallflowers*

*Above: Traditionally, the front gardens of old cottages did not have a lawn, but were completely filled with a carpet of flowers, leaving just a path to the door.*

*Right: Hardy cranesbills, mallows, roses and lady's mantle are all at home in a cottage garden. Rejuvenate clumps of perennial plants every few years.*

## Scented foliage

Herbs
Lavender
Salvia grahamii
*(blackcurrant scent)*
Salvia rutilans *(pineapple scent)*
*Scented-leaved pelargoniums
(various citrus, spice, balsam,
rose and pine scents)*

*Below: Herbs and roses - a cottagey
combination chosen for scents and
colors. The herbal scents are released
when the leaves are brushed, so plant
herbs towards the front of the border.*

# Scented borders

Scent is one of the most overlooked assets of a flower garden, yet by choosing carefully it is possible to have a constantly changing perfumed accompaniment to a walk round the garden. Seating areas are particularly good places for perfumed plants, or they could be used as the inspiration for an entire fragrant garden. Scented plants come in two basic types; those with perfumed flowers and those with aromatic leaves. Choose some of each for a succession of scents. Flowers deliver their perfume all the time they are fully open and some, such as lilies, only last a short time. Some of the best scented flowers have the most uninteresting blooms - you would hardly notice night-scented stock and sweet rocket, so tuck them in with more spectacular but unscented displays. Modern cultivars of old scented favorites, such as flowering tobacco and many roses, have lost much of their scent - choose old-fashioned kinds where possible. Use fragrant flowers in distinct groups all round the garden, so that their scents do not overlap. Aromatic leaves need to be bruised to release their fragrance, so place them where you can brush past them. Since scent is easily dispersed on the breeze, choose a sheltered, preferably enclosed, site for scented plants. Although many plants are scented during the day, most produce their strongest scent in the evening to attract night-flying insects for pollination. Scent will also be strongest when the air is warm and humid.

*Above: Not all roses are heavily
perfumed, but one of the best is
this 'Fragrant Cloud', a hybrid tea.
Check rose catalogs for details of
other well-scented kinds.*

## Scented flowers

Cosmos atrosanguineus
*(chocolate-scented cosmos)*
Dianthus *(pinks)*
Hesperis matronalis
*(sweet rocket)*
*Honeysuckle, Hyacinths*
Jasminum officinale *(Jasmine)*
*Lavender,* Lilium regale,
candidum *and some lily hybrids*
Nicotiana affinis
*(flowering tobacco)*
*Night-scented stock*
Roses, Stocks
*(Brompton or East Lothian)*
Sweet peas
Wallflowers

**Above:** Nicotiana alata *is well known for scenting the evening garden. Few modern varieties are strongly scented; try* 'Fragrant Cloud' *and the tall* Nicotiana sylvestris; *both white.*

**Above:** *Pinks and lavenders; both the foliage and flowers of lavender are scented; this cultivar is a form of French lavender with large petals,* Lavandula stoechas *'Pendunculata'*

**Right:** Santolina chamaecyparissus *(cotton lavender) has silvery foliage that smells attractively herbal when bruised. Victorian ladies brushed their clothes with it to repel moths.*

# Themed borders

*Above: Yellow* Potentilla, Achillea, *hollyhock and* Helichrysum *flowers combine well with green, blue-gray, silver and cream-variegated foliage.*

*Below: This restful border features* Knautia macedonica, Lathyrus latifolius, *tree mallow,* Salvia superba, Bergenia *and* Dahlia *'Rutland Water'.*

Pastel color themes of pinks, mauves and purples have long been firm favorites in the garden, but now there is an increasing trend for much more limited color schemes. These are usually based on one color, such as white, plus every possible foliage color - variegated, gold, gray, silver, blue and every shade of green. Rather than turn an entire small garden over to such an extreme style, it is much better to make over an individual bed. And instead of using a single color, which is very difficult to do well, it is much better to use a slightly broader color scheme. A 'blue' garden could, for example, contain purple, lilac and blue flowers. This avoids the difficulty of finding enough different true blue flowers to fill the space, and the slight variation of shades adds depth and interest without straying too far from the chosen color scheme. Similarly, a 'yellow' garden could contain cream, buff-orange, and earthy ocher colors, as well as true yellows - a yellow garden looks particularly good with plenty of lime green and gold-variegated foliage added, too. Regardless of the colors you choose, the great trick is to select plants whose shape and texture contrast well together. Avoid anything bland, and go instead for spiky or strap-shaped foliage, huge architectural shapes, bold upright spires, neat hummocks, dense spreading ground cover dotted with flowers, arching stems, frothy flowers, prickles, globes and other strong shapes.

*Right: Both the flowers and leaves of* Eryngium alpinum *have harsh, spiky shapes. These are exactly the sort of striking architectural forms that are invaluable in a color schemed garden.*

**Above:** *Red borders are great fun though not easy to get 'right'. Here, shades of purplish-red are used throughout, with an enormous range of leaf and flower shapes and sizes.*

**Right:** *A cool white spring border, with three cultivars of white tulips in front of a fragrant viburnum. White pansies nestle among the foliage of variegated hostas, silver artemisia,* Stachys lanata, *green iris and box.*

# Container roses

1 *Dig a planting hole about twice the size of the pot in which the rose is growing. The soil should be well dug over and manured.*

2 *Put a spadeful of well-rotted manure into the hole and mix it in with the soil, so that the rose roots grow into good, retentive soil.*

3 *Sprinkle a handful of general-purpose or rose fertilizer over the base of the hole; mix it well into the soil.*

4 *The rose should have been well watered on the previous day. Tip it carefully out of its pot without breaking up the ball of roots.*

Compact roses, sold under the general name of patio roses, make good plants for tubs in any sunny spot. Bush plants are most often seen, but short standards can look very effective amongst a display of shorter plants. This technique is particularly stunning when used for spreading cultivars, such as 'Nozomi', which produces a small weeping tree when grown as a standard. Miniature roses can also be grown in containers, but being slightly more tender are best moved under cover for winter in all but the mildest regions. Otherwise, overwinter potted roses by sinking the pot to its rim in vacant soil in a garden bed, or by lagging it with hessian or old newspaper. Be sure to prevent the soil in the pot from freezing solid, which damages the roots. Prune container roses in the usual way, but less severely; with miniature roses, remove any dead twigs and slightly thin out cluttered growth. Because the roots are confined in a pot, feed container roses regularly during spring and summer with a liquid rose food. Water during the growing season, but do not allow pots to become waterlogged in winter. Container roses planted in a soil-based potting mix can remain in the same pot for two to three years. Then either replant the rose into a garden bed or move it to a larger pot with fresh potting mixture in early spring.

**Right:** *Remove the individual heads of floribunda roses, such as this 'Korresia', when they are over. Cut the whole stem back about 12in (30cm), just above a growth bud for more flowers.*

**5** Position the rose with its best 'side' facing out front and the top of the rootball level with the soil surface.

**6** Fill in the planting hole around the rootball. Use improved topsoil made by mixing the border soil with a little more well-rotted manure and a sprinkling of fertilizer.

**7** Firm the new soil lightly down. Add more soil to bring the level back flush with the surrounding area.

**8** Mulch with a 2in(5cm)-deep circle of well-rotted manure. Start 2in (5cm) from the stem, extending out 18in(45cm).

**9** Finally, water the plant in well, concentrating the water near the stem and around the edge of the rootball. Continue to water the rose thoroughly right through the first season whenever the soil is dry.

77

# A rose border

Nurseries and garden centers now stock a wider selection of roses than ever. Modern bush roses flower from early summer until the fall, and include the hybrid teas and floribundas, also known as large-flowered and cluster-flowered roses. Miniature roses grow to about 12-24in(30-60cm) tall, while patio roses are about halfway in size between miniature and bush roses, and ideal for containers. Ground cover roses are prostrate, but it is difficult to weed around them, as their stems are so prickly. However, grown on upright stems as short standards, they are spectacular, creating a waterfall of flowers. Old-fashioned shrub roses are grown for their classic scent and charming old-world colors. They are bush roses but often a bit straggly and in need of support; most only flower in early summer though some kinds have occasional flowers later too. Nowadays, some modern roses, such as the New English roses) are bred to look like old roses but with the long flowering season of modern kinds - the best of both worlds. Traditionally, roses were grown in beds of their own with bare soil underneath, while modern bush roses look good grown with a carpet of annual flowers. Old-fashioned roses look best treated like any flowering shrubs and grown in a mixed border of cottage garden flowers or herbaceous plants, particularly those that flower after the roses are over.

*Left: Herbs are good for the front of a border of roses where the soil gets dry. Here, 'Graham Thomas', one of the New English roses, teams effectively with the purple-leaved sage.*

*Left: Standard and half-standard roses add height to a border without taking up too much space. This is Rosa 'Excelsa', a once-flowering rambler that can attain a height of 20ft(6m).*

*Below: Modern roses are all too rarely used as flowering shrubs in mixed borders. Here, 'Masquerade', a floribunda, mingles with* Campanula, Alchemilla *and other border plants.*

*Left: Arches or pillars are useful for accommodating climbing roses, such as 'Veilchenblau' and 'Compte de Chambord', shown here, and help to make the border look tall and solid.*

*Below: Miniature roses are often mistaken for houseplants, but they are outdoor varieties and require the same care as their larger cousins. This red variety is called 'Royal Baby'.*

*Left: Violets make superb ground cover under roses, as they thrive in light shade and do not compete for nutrients. This old moss rose, 'Jean Bodin', is planted with* Viola cornuta. *Violets self-seed readily, and soon create their own carpet. Plant them 1in(2.5cm) apart.*

# Flowers for dry shade

Some gardens are in almost permanent shade due to the presence of large overhanging trees or nearby buildings, but even relatively normal gardens often have 'problem' corners in between walls or fences where the sun never reaches. In these situations, shade is very often associated with dry soil. This is because tree branches or nearby structures deflect rainwater away, so less than normal falls on the soil. In addition, both trees and walls draw a great deal of moisture up from the soil. So the first rule when tackling a dry shady area is to add as much well-rotted organic matter as possible to improve the soil's water-holding capacity. If tree roots are close to the surface, do not try to dig in organic matter. Instead, use it the way it arrives naturally in woodland - spread a thick layer over the soil surface. Worms will gradually drag it down, and an annual top-up is all that is needed to keep a deep, moisture-retaining mulch in which suitable plants will thrive. Which are suitable? Well, if you plant 'normal' flowers in a dark situation, they simply grow tall thin stems that break easily, and unnaturally large foliage that is very prone to attack by pests and diseases. Worst of all, they will not flower. The answer is to plant dry shade-tolerant kinds. Some plants do, in fact, grow better in shade than anywhere else. Typically, shade-loving plants are not the most colorful ones, so it is no good expecting a riot of color. However, you can create a cool, sophisticated and charming display, which is much more suited to shady conditions.

Bergenia cordifolia

### Flowers for dry shade

Alchemilla mollis
Arum italicum 'Pictum'
Bergenia
Brunnera macrophylla
Digitalis purpurea (foxglove)
Epimedium
Euphorbia robbiae
Hypericum 'Hidcote'
Iris foetidissima
Lamium (ornamental deadnettle)
Lunaria annua (honesty)
Liriope muscari
Pachysandra terminalis
Vinca (periwinkle)
Viola labradorica

Alchemilla mollis
(lady's mantle)

Even plants suited to growing in dry shade, such as the ones featured here, need to be kept watered in dry weather after planting. Continue to water them until they are well established.

Asperula odorata
(sweet woodruff)

**Left:** *Honesty flowers in its second year and then dies. Leave the plants to self-seed. Variegated forms, such as this* Lunaria annua *'Alba Variegata', only develop variegation in the second year. Save the dried seedheads to use in winter flower arrangements.*

**Right:** Liriope muscari *(turf lily) is not very well known, but it is a useful and pretty, compact, clump-forming, low plant for dry shade. It flowers late in the season. Allow the clumps to spread; do not lift and divide them until it is absolutely necessary.*

Vinca major 'Variegata' (periwinkle)

Geranium phaeum

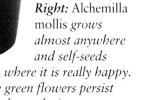

Viola labradorica 'Purpurea'

**Right:** Alchemilla mollis *grows almost anywhere and self-seeds where it is really happy. The lime green flowers persist for several months in summer, and the pleated leaves are attractive for most of the year.*

# Flowers for sun and poor soil

On the face of it, a sunny site should be one of the easiest to choose plants for, and when the soil is deep, fertile and stays reasonably moist, the majority of annual bedding plants and herbaceous flowers will indeed do very well. But problems arise when the soil is thin, poor and dries out severely, and the site gets very hot. This commonly happens in front of a wall that faces the sun, although it can also be true of a small courtyard garden surrounded by walls that reflect the heat. Here, you must choose plants with great care. Unless you are prepared to improve the soil and water it regularly, avoid plants that simply need well-drained conditions; in most cases, they need soil that does not stay wet for long but does not dry out severely either. Opt for known heat- and drought-tolerant kinds and do not add a great deal of organic matter and fertilizer - these sorts of plants do not like it. They need hard conditions if they are to give of their best.

Generally speaking, perennial plants and bulbs are safest in this situation, as once they are established, they virtually look after themselves. However, if you grow heat-loving annuals (the ones with succulent leaves and whose flowers only open in sun), you will need to water them for some weeks after planting, as they will only tolerate the conditions when safely established. Drought-tolerant annuals are certainly the plants to choose for containers in this situation.

*Right:* Senecio 'Sunshine' (previously Senecio greyii) has tough, gray, felty leaves that prevent the plant losing too much water in dry conditions. Use it as an effective foliar foil to more colorful sunloving plants.

Cistus pulverulentus 'Sunset'

Dianthus (pinks)

Anacyclus depressus

Armeria maritima 'Alba'

Lavandula angustifolia
'Munstead'

Eryngium planum

Sempervivum
arachnoideum

Armeria maritima
'Rubra'

## Plants for poor soil in a hot sunny spot

Acaena *(New Zealand burr)*
Armeria maritima *(thrift)*
Eremurus *(foxtail lily)*
Eryngium *(sea holly)*
Euphorbia cyparissias
E. polychroma, E. wulfenii
Gladiolus papilio
Helianthemum
Helichrysum amorghenum
H. angustifolium
Iris unguicularis
*(winter-flowering iris)*
Lampranthus *(use as annual)*
Leucanthemum hosmariense
Mesembryanthemum *(as annual)*
Nerine bowdenii
Portulaca *(as annual)*, Sedum
Sempervivum *(houseleek)*
Verbascum bombyciferum

**Below:** Allium sphaerocephalon *is a useful drought-tolerant summer-flowering bulb for planting in groups between shrubs. There is no need to lift the bulbs after they have flowered, as they are quite hardy.*

# Flowers for rock gardens

Rock gardens are raised beds created deliberately to provide extremely well-drained conditions for plants from a mountainous native habitat. A thick layer of gravel and broken rocks on the surface of the bed allows fleshy plants to rest on a fast-drying surface to avoid rotting, and a high proportion of gravel in the soil beneath means that surface water runs away fast. However, a well-planned rock garden should not become bone dry in summer. The ideal rock garden soil is well drained but moisture retentive. This is easily achieved by mixing topsoil, gritty sand and gravel, and a low-nutrient form of organic matter (such as peat or coir) in roughly equal quantities. Rock plants are best planted in early spring, which gives them some time to establish before summer sun dries out the top of the bed too much. However, plants can be put in even when in flower, provided you water them for the first few months. Like other plants, rock plants vary in the amount of bright sun they like. Relatively few tolerate searing hot sun all day long - most prefer a few hours shade cast by nearby rocks or bigger plants. Choose a mixture of plant shapes and sizes for best effect, and aim for a long flowering season by selecting plants and bulbs that flower in succession from spring onwards.

Saxifraga 'Fleece'

Aubretia ' Blue Down'

Silene 'Druett's Variegated'

Viola 'Molly Sanderson'

Saxifraga 'Cloth of Gold'

Primula auricula

Oxalis adenophylla

Sempervivum 'Commander Hay'

Raoulia australis

Saxifraga 'Peter Pan'

**1** Spring is a good time to remedy any gaps in an existing rock garden. Before adding a new plant to the bed, carefully scrape away the topdressing of grit from the planting site using a narrow-bladed trowel.

**2** Dig out a hole slightly larger than the pot in which the new plant is growing. Put the excess soil in a bucket so that it does not make the surrounding topdressing dirty.

Arabis fernandii-coburgii *'Variegata'*

Aubretia *'Red Carpet'*

Aubretia *'Astola'*

Aubretia *'Blue Mist'*

Saxifraga *'Silver Cushion'*

Saxifraga *'Finding'*

Arenaria balearica

Saxifraga cotyledon *'Southside Seedling'*

Saxifraga aizoon *'Balcana'*

**4** Replace the gritty topdressing around the new plant. This immediately makes it blend in with surrounding plants, and by working the grit well under the collar of the plant you help to prevent neck rot.

**5** While obvious gaps need filling, leave an area of clear gravel round distinct groups of plants as this helps to show them off advantageously.

**3** Knock the new plant carefully out of its pot and plant it into the prepared hole. To allow the new roots to grow into the ground, break up the soil at the base of the hole.

85

# Planting through gravel

When there is not enough time to look after a conventional flower garden, a gravel garden may be just the answer. Here, appropriate flowers are grown through a deep layer of gravel, which acts as a permanent mulch, smothering weeds out and keeping moisture in. A gravel garden can be created from a tiny town courtyard garden or as a feature within a large area of paving or patio, but it is a good way to use a small front garden, particularly one that has to double up as car parking space occasionally.

To make a gravel garden, first strip the ground of turf - you can lay gravel around any large plants or shrubs you wish to keep. For a real no-labor garden, lay a sheet of slitted black plastic or special woven plastic landscape fabric over the area and then cover it with 2in(5cm) of gravel. This effectively prevents any weeds, and also stops flowers seeding themselves between the stones. Put in plants where required by brushing the gravel aside, cutting crosses in the plastic and planting through the holes. Otherwise, spread gravel straight over the leveled soil; a few weeds will get through, but flowers will be free to seed themselves. Simply weed out any that are not wanted. Choosing the right plants is a vital part of creating a gravel garden; aim for a Mediterranean look, full of spiky shapes and aromatic foliage plants, and decorate it with giant cobblestones and chunks of rock, alpine sink gardens and a range of terracotta pots to make the most of this unique ambience.

## Plants for gravel gardens

Alchemilla mollis
Acanthus
Agapanthus
Artemisia
*Artichoke*
*Bamboo*
Crocosmia
Euphorbia wulfenii
*Junipers*
Hemerocallis
Kniphofia
Liatris
*Ornamental sages*
Phormium
*Rosemary*
Verbascum
Yucca

1 Cover the soil with perforated black plastic or landscape fabric. If necessary, secure it with bent wire prongs pushed through into the soil to prevent billowing in a breeze.

2 Spread a 2in(5cm)-thick layer of gravel evenly over the plastic. Pea gravel with rounded edges looks best. If the gravel comes from the seabed, wash it first to remove the salt.

3 When you have decided where you wish to put in a plant, scrape back the gravel to reveal the plastic. Leave the spare gravel nearby as it will be replaced after planting.

**4** Make two cuts crossing each other in the middle of the planting site, each one about twice the diameter of the pot to allow room for working.

**5** Peel back the corners of the plastic to expose the soil beneath; place stones or gravel on the flaps to hold them back while you plant.

**6** Scoop out soil from the planting hole with a small trowel. If the soil was not first prepared for planting, dig a larger hole and add organic matter.

**7** When the plant is out of its pot, make sure the planting hole is large enough for the rootball. Sit it in position, with its best side to the front.

**8** Fill in the space around the rootball with soil and firm down lightly. Water well and then push back the plastic flaps, so that they fit snugly around the plant.

**9** Holding the plant over to one side, sweep the spare gravel back round the plant with your hand, so that all the plastic is completely hidden.

**10** Now the plant looks as if it has grown up naturally through the gravel. Plant large-growing subjects on their own; smaller kinds are best grouped together for greater effect.

Helianthemum 'Sunbeam'

# Gravel garden borders

You can grow all kinds of plants in gravel: heat-loving, drought-tolerant flowers, such as red hot pokers, *Euphorbia wulfenii* and ornamental sages, are a popular choice, as they provide year-round effect. (They are also useful if the gravel area doubles as extra car parking space; plants of this size are easy to see and you can avoid driving over them.) However, many smaller flowers, such as spreading rock plants, hardy annuals and even wallflowers, are also happy growing in gravel. Where the gravel is placed over soil, they will often self-seed freely, creating attractive natural effects. Then, instead of just using gravel as a permanent mulch over flower beds, you could create a complete gravel garden, in which plants spread and self-seed, leaving meandering paths of clear gravel between groups. With a garden of this type, you often have to clear seedlings from pathways to make room to walk through once it is well established. This can make a very attractive, low-maintenance, natural or cottage-style garden, but do clear all perennial weeds out of the ground first. For a more formal garden, you could plant trailing

*Above:* Bergenia 'Beethoven'. *Bergenia flowers, usually pink, mauve or red, appear in late winter and spring. The leaves are large and evergreen.*

annuals, such as nasturtiums or ornamental gourds, in beds on either side of a gravel walk and allow them to trail forwards over the path. This softens the hard edges of a gravel path under planted fruit tunnels or around the edge of a patio. Try a similar technique to make a slightly raised scree garden, using chunks of rock and gravel planted with choicer alpine flowers. In all but the smallest areas, sink stone slabs into the surface as 'stepping stones' to provide a firm surface for walking on or when weeding. The 2in(5cm)-deep mulch of gravel over already well-drained soil provides ideal growing conditions and allows plants to set seed to provide their own replacements.

**1** Create a mini 'island bed' in a graveled area by grouping several warmth-loving and fairly drought-tolerant plants together. Make a separate planting hole for each one.

**2** For the best effect, choose plants with different flower shapes and heights, and plant the tallest at the center and the shortest to the sides and front. Offer up the plants first to see how they will look.

**Left:** *Being summer-dormant, spring bulbs team up well with other plants that tolerate hot, dry summers. Here, they combine with Euphorbia wulfenii, a singularly striking architectural plant for any gravel garden display.*

**4** This scheme would look equally at home in a cottage garden or a car parking area covered with gravel. In the latter case, roughly surround the plants with large stones as an early warning!

**Above:** *Many rock plants are good subjects; these are* Linum arboreum *and* Erinus alpinus. *The gravel mulch smothers out weeds and helps the soil to retain moisture.*

Osteospermum 'Stardust'

Armeria formosa

Lavandula 'Munstead Dwarf'

Stachys lanata

**3** Continue adding plants, including some prostrate kinds that spill forwards over the gravel, so that it looks as if the plants had seeded themselves.

Helianthemum 'Sunbeam'

Nepeta mussinii

89

# Flowers for damp soil

Some kinds of soil are notorious for remaining damp for most of the year. They include heavy clay soils, peaty fenland soils, and those in low-lying areas. If you try and grow most 'normal' plants here, their roots are likely to rot, especially in winter. There are various ways round the problem of damp soil. One is to grow plants such as lilies, that are likely to rot if kept too wet in winter, in pots. These can be sunk to their rims into the ground in early summer, then taken up in the fall and stored in a cold frame with a deep gravel base for drainage during the winter. Another alternative is to improve the soil as much as possible, then only grow summer annuals. However, both techniques make a great deal of work. Provided the ground is not actually waterlogged (in which case bog plants are the answer, see page 92), the simplest solution is to grow moisture-loving plants. Most of these need sun for at least half the day, although there are some that are suitable for shadier conditions. It is also advisable to improve the soil. If the soil is heavy clay, dig in plenty of well-rotted organic matter plus gritty sand (the sort sold in garden centers as potting sand). Allow a bucketful or more per square yard/meter. Highly organic soils such as peaty fenland kinds are best improved with gritty sand, and low-lying areas are best raised up by adding a mixture of good topsoil, organic matter and grit. Aim to raise the soil at least a few inches above that of surrounding areas so that surplus moisture has somewhere to run away to. If it is possible, also try to dig a drainage channel leading off to a ditch, so that surface water will run away faster after heavy rain.

Geum rivale
(water avens)

Geum
'Lady Stratheden'

Geum borisii

Geum
'Mrs J. Bradshaw'

## Flowers for moist soil

Anemone japonica
Astilbe
Dierama *(angel's fishing rod)*
Filipendula
Geum
Hosta
Inula
Ligularia
Lobelia cardinalis
Lythrum
Primroses
Primula
Ranunculus ficaria
*(cultivated celandines)*
Rodgersia
*Solomon's seal*
Thalictrum

**Right:** *Astilbes are good summer flowering perennials for damp soil in a sunny or lightly shaded spot. This is Astilbe x arendsii 'Hyacinth', but many named hybrids are available.*

Primula japonica 'Postford White'

Primula x 'Geisha Girl'

Primula veris *(cowslip)*

Primula pulverulenta

Primula japonica

Primula chungensis

**Left:** *Wild and cultivated geums are all useful, long-flowering plants for a damp border. The wild Geum rivale tolerates shade, but cultivated kinds prefer more sun.*

**Right:** *Primulas flower mainly in late spring and early summer. Provide them with soil that never dries out, and sun or slight shade, depending on species. The nurseries' plant care label will give details.*

Primula vulgaris flore plena 'Dawn Ansell'

# Flowers for waterside planting and bog gardens

Waterlogged soil can be a real problem, as it is very difficult to improve conditions enough to permit normal plants to grow happily. The only way to have a reasonably conventional garden is to make raised beds. Raise the sides by at least 12in(30cm) and preferably 24-36in(60-90cm) above ground, and fill the bed itself with a mixture of good topsoil, gritty sand and organic matter. Raised beds work particularly successfully over permanently wet soil, as plants will grow in well-drained soil, but their roots can always find water. However, if you do not wish to go to the trouble and expense of creating raised beds, the best approach is to make a bog garden and grow plants whose natural habitat is standing in water. Using bog plants, you can make the most of a naturally wet or sunken area of the garden or a natural streamside. Bog plants are also good planted round a pond where you want a natural effect. If the ground is not naturally boggy, excavate a 12in(30cm) deep depression and line it with black plastic or pond liner, and fill it with plain garden soil. The bog garden should be slightly lower than the pond; if water runs off from the bog garden into the pond it is likely to make the water turn green. The sort of plants that enjoy bog garden conditions are those that are commonly sold for planting in shallow water round the edges of ponds, so they associate particularly well with water. Some bog garden plants look like cultivated versions of wild flowers, with habits to match. But some, particularly the water iris, are delightful and highly collectable plants to be treasured.

1 Excavate an informally shaped depression, about 12in(30cm) deep, to give a natural-looking bed. You could, perhaps, take advantage of a natural dip in the garden.

4 Place a 1-2in(2.5-5cm) layer of gravel in the base to facilitate drainage. Bog garden soil needs to be moist but not totally under water.

## Flowers for boggy soil

Cardamine pratensis 'Flore Pleno' (double lady's smock)
Caltha palustris
(kingcup, marsh marigold)
Gunnera manicata
Houttuynia cordata
Iris fulvala, I. laevigata
(water iris), I. pseudacorus,
I. versicolor, Lythrum
Lysichitum americanum
(bog arum)
Menyanthes trifoliata (bog bean)
Mimulus (monkey musk)
Peltiphyllum peltatum
Scrophularia aquatica 'Variegata'
(variegated water figwort)
Trollius x cultorum
(globeflower)
Zantedeschia aethiopica
(arum lily)

**Right:** *A typical bog garden plant grouping:* Trollius, Hosta *and* Ligularia *with the variegated grass* Glyceria maxima 'Variegata'.

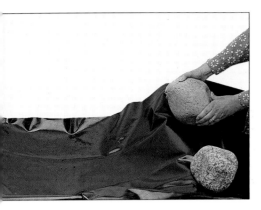

**2** *Lay a sheet of thick black plastic over the depression and hold it in place with stones at each corner to prevent billowing while you work.*

**3** *Perforate the lowest part of the liner. The easiest way to do this is using a garden fork. The holes will allow surplus water to drain away.*

**5** *Sink perforated hosepipe through the gravel, leaving the unperforated end out above the edge of the bog garden for watering during dry spells.*

**6** *Fill the bog garden up with a mixture of border soil and organic matter, such as old growing bag potting mixture or garden soil.*

*Above: Bog garden plants, such as Rheum (ornamental rhubarb) and Rodgersia, associate well with a pond, and thrive in damp marginal soils.*

**7** *Saturate the soil with water. The weight of the water will make the liner sink into the depression. Now you are ready to plant up the bed.*

Iris pallida 'Variegata' makes an attractive foliage plant after the flowers are over.

*Left:* Mimulus, Polygonum *and* Iris pallida *'Variegata' in boggy ground around a lily pond create a natural background. Bog plants generally need sun for most of the day to thrive.*

# Planting up a bog garden

The best time to plant up a bog garden is in spring, although you can add new plants during the summer, provided they are pot grown. Since many of the most easily available bog garden plants flower in spring and early summer (primulas, marsh marigolds, irises, mimulus, astilbe) it pays to include some that will keep the display going well into late summer or early fall. *Eupatorium* (hemp agrimony), *Lythrum*, *Lobelia cardinalis*, *L. syphilitica* and *Schizostylis* (kaffir lily) are all useful additions. Bog gardens need regular maintenance. Apart from the usual weeds, some bog garden plants, particularly the wilder ones such as water figwort, seed themselves rather freely, so remove surplus seedlings before they become a nuisance. Hand weeding is best, as bog garden plants quickly cover the ground, making hoeing risky, and if the area is lined with plastic you risk tearing the liner, leading to excess drainage. Removing dead flowering stems in good time prevents the appearance of unwanted seedlings, but leave teasel seedheads for the birds to enjoy. Avoid using fertilizers, especially if wildflowers are included in the planting or if the bog garden is close to a pond, where run-off may make the water go green. Slugs and snails are the worst pests of bog gardens, as they thrive in moist conditions and are specially attracted to hostas and primulas. Slugs may not be a problem if frogs breed in a nearby pond, as they feed on them. Snails can be difficult to control. The best solution is a physical barrier round the outer edges of the bog garden or a ring of thinly scattered slug pellets or slug tape, which needs renewing frequently. Alternatively avoid 'at risk' plants and concentrate on tougher-leaved species.

*1 Make a hole the same size as the pot in which your chosen plant is growing. Knock the plant out of its pot and sit it in place.*

*2 Plants look best grouped together in small 'cameos'. The spaces between the groups help to set them off and leave room for stones or gravel.*

*3 Choose plants with a wide range of forms - tall, upright shapes and dumpy rounded ones, and a mix of flowers and foliage. Hostas are ideal.*

**4** Tuck smooth, rounded pebbles between the groups of plants for color and texture contrast and to show up the plants.

**5** Fit a small funnel to the end of the perforated hosepipe that is buried under the soil. Pour water down the funnel until the soil is evenly wet.

**Above:** Mimulus luteus *(monkey musk)* can get out of control in time, so thin out excess growth periodically in spring and summer.

**6** The finished planting scheme looks attractive straightaway. After about three years, the clumps of plants will have become overcrowded. Dig them up and divide them in early spring.

Lysimachia thyrsiflora

Hosta

Mimulus

Astilbe

Lobelia cardinalis

Primula veris

95

# Flower lawns

Flower lawns are charming, but do not consider them as an alternative to normal grass lawns, as they cannot stand much wear. Instead, think of them as decorative, and often scented, floral features that contribute a change of surface to part of a conventional garden, and on which you can occasionally stand or sit - like a rug you keep for special occasions indoors. Use a flower lawn to surround a seat or sundial, as a low-maintenance ground cover bed, or on a bank that you do not want to mow. Suitable plants for flower lawns all need a sunny situation and light, well-drained soil. If your soil is not suitable, use an edging of stone or bricks to build a slightly raised bed - perhaps 6in (15cm) above ground level - and fill this with a mixture of good topsoil and grit. Plant through 2in(5cm) or so of coarse gravel, and the plants should thrive. Naturally low, ground-hugging species, such as chamomile (the non-flowering form 'Treneague') and prostrate thymes are traditional choices, but slightly taller carpeting plants, such as heathers are also suitable. (Heathers need more organic matter, and unless you choose lime-tolerant species, make sure they have acid soil.) Alpine flower lawns were once in vogue; these used a mixture of prostrate and mound-shaped plants growing in a gravelly soil, with a mulch of pea shingle between plants, rather like a modern scree garden, but with 'wall to wall' plants. If you want to walk through a flower lawn regularly without damaging the plants, lay paths of bark chippings or 'stepping stones' for a pretty but practical effect. A real flower lawn has no other decorative features, but there is no reason why you should not add chunks of rock to an alpine lawn, silver birch logs to a heather lawn, or plants in containers to a herb lawn. As an interesting variation on a flower lawn, why not create a herbal seat. To do this, make a knee-high raised bed from brick or stone blocks, with back and armrests of the same material, film the 'seat' with soil and plant it with creeping flowers and herbs.

*Below: An informal thyme lawn made of Thymus drucei. Stone 'stepping stones' have been laid to enable people to cross the lawn without damaging the plants. Set prostrate thymes about 12in(30cm) apart to form a reasonably fast cover; propagate your own from cuttings for economy.*

*Thymus drucei (syn. Thymus praecox articus) forms a 2in(5cm) deep carpet with aromatic foliage and purple to mauve flowers in summer.*

## Plants for flower lawns

Ajuga reptans
*Creeping thymes*
Dianthus alpinus *cultivars*
Erinus alpinus
Erodium reichardii
Geranium *'Ballerina' and 'Lawrence Flatman'*
*Mossy saxifrages*
Phlox adsurgens *cultivars*
*Prostrate rosemary*
Sagina glabra *'Aurea'*
Sedum acre
Trifolium repens *'Purpurascens Quadrifolium' (purple four-leaved clover)*

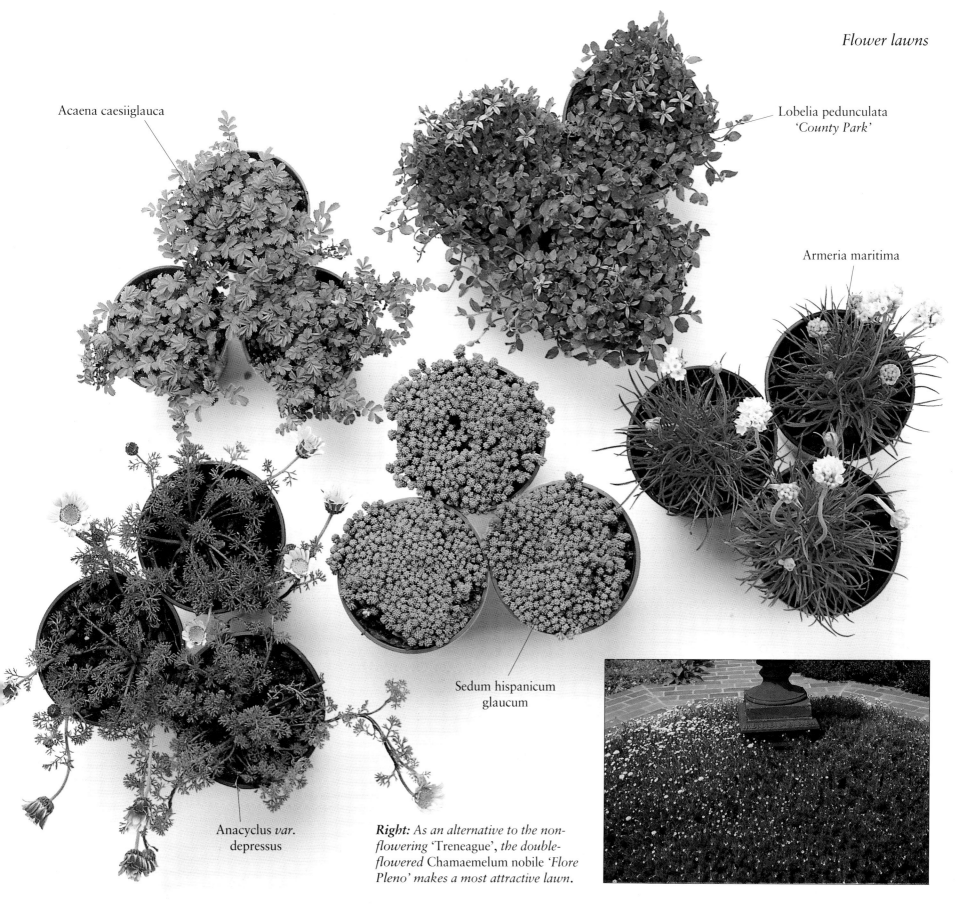

Acaena caesiiglauca

Lobelia pedunculata
'*County Park*'

Armeria maritima

Sedum hispanicum
glaucum

Anacyclus *var.*
depressus

**Right:** *As an alternative to the non-flowering* 'Treneague', *the double-flowered* Chamaemelum nobile '*Flore Pleno*' *makes a most attractive lawn.*

# Wildflower areas

As gardens become more ecologically aware, wildflowers are increasingly joining their cultivated cousins. It is possible to create very attractive gardens entirely from wildflowers, using various species in place of cultivated plants in relatively normal garden schemes. But, more popular, is a separate wildlife area at the bottom of the garden. If the aim is to attract wildlife, a pond is essential, ideally one with shallow sides so that creatures can get in and out. The pond itself creates a good habitat for aquatic plants, and the surrounding area, if damp, makes a good place to grow waterside wildflowers. Trees and shrubs are another essential, as in order to attract birds, you need to provide them with places to perch and nest. Choose species that provide fruits and berries as an added attraction. Wildflowers can take up the remaining space.

Wildflower plants are rarely available and then only in a limited range of species; so it is best to grow your own plants from seed. Seed firms provide both individual species and mixtures suitable for growing in all the various situations you may encounter - shade, grassland, under hedges, etc. Do not simply scatter wildflower seed onto the ground where you want plants to colonize; it does not work. Treat them like hardy annuals and sow them in rows in a bit of spare ground, then transplant them. Or sow them in trays of seed potting mixture and pot them on when they are big enough. For a wildflower lawn, mix wildflower and grass seed together, then sow like a normal lawn. Once a good stand of wild flowers is established, it will self-seed and provide replacements. Do not use fertilizers, and avoid cutting wildflower lawns until late summer, when seeds will have been shed. Remove any weed species.

**Right:** *The snakeshead fritillary thrives in damp soil and light shade. It is ideal for naturalizing under trees in a moist garden or light woodland, or in shade near a wild pond.*

Lychnis flos-cuculi
*(ragged robin)*

Primula vulgaris
*(primrose)*

Primula veris
*(Cowslip)*

Viola labradorica
*(violet)*

Fritillaria meleagris
*(Snakeshead fritillary)*

Geum rivale
*(water avens)*

Pulsatilla vulgaris
*(Pasque flower)*

Viola labradorica
*(violet)*

*1* To *create a wildflower lawn, mix suitable species into grass seed or buy a ready mixed wildflower lawn seed. The best time to sow is in spring or fall.*

*Stir well before sowing, as flower seed, being smaller, will sink to the bottom.*

*2* *Sprinkle the seed mixture over previously dug, raked and leveled soil, but do not use any fertilizer. Fertilizers encourage the grass to grow but discourage the wildflowers.*

*3* *After sowing (about 1-2oz per yd²/ 28-56gm per m²) rake the seed in lightly so that most of it is covered. Water well and keep watered in dry weather until the grass is through.*

# Flower carpets

Low, ground-hugging flowers look great planted as a carpet under trees and shrubs. To create the carpet effect, either use the same plant right across the border or mix different colors together (perhaps using several similar plants) for more of a 'Persian carpet' effect. A flowering carpet not only helps to set off the flowers above, but also creates a feeling of continuity, which visually pulls together a large border. It can also be a useful way of creating interest when the 'top tier' is out of season. For instance, under a predominately summer-flowering shrub border you could have a carpet of spring flowers, such as *Anemone blanda*, snowdrops or early-flowering dwarf narcissi (all of which tolerate light shade). Under a border that looks best in spring, choose flowers that look colorful all summer, such as *Impatiens,* which again tolerates light shade. If you want to use annual flowers such as *Alyssum* that need more sun, then keep the carpet towards the front of the border where there is more light. Sun-loving plants in deep shade will grow spindly and do not flower. Alternatively, use a carpet of one of the really ground-hugging hardy cranesbills to lend continuity right across the border. In the fall, a carpet of hardy cyclamen, fall crocus or colchicums looks utterly striking beneath a border filled with fall foliage colors.

Although flowering carpets are usually used to contrast with shrubs, there is no reason why you should not use the same idea in a border of tall, herbaceous flowers. Try low, shade-loving plants, such as hostas, *Lamium* (ornamental deadnettle) or *Pulmonaria,* for example. In an annual border, use a low carpet of *Impatiens* or try *Begonia semperflorens,* already in flower, to contrast with tall plants and striking shapes.

*In light woodland or mixed borders* Anemone blanda *makes a good substitute for the wild wood anemone. The corms have no right way up; to plant them, just drop them into small holes.*

***Above:*** *A continuous cover of one kind of flower can also look very striking. Here,* Anemone blanda *has been naturalized around summer-flowering shrubs for spring color.*

***Left:*** *A mixed carpet of spring-flowering bulbs for shady conditions, such as you find in light woodland or beneath shrubs in a border: dog's-tooth violet* (Erythronium), *wood anemones and* Anemone blanda.

***Right:*** Cyclamen coum *thrives in short grass under trees and makes a splash of color in early spring. Large colonies gradually build up by self-seeding.*

# Flowers for light woodland

Light dappled shade will support many flowers that dislike strong direct sun, particularly those that prefer moist soil. In light woodland, hardy cyclamen, trillium, dog's tooth violet and Solomon's seal thrive in diffuse light and a soil rich in leafmold. In a shrub border, herbaceous and other flowers, such as hellebores, lily of the valley, dicentra and hostas, will do well. Choose a mixture of low ground-hugging plants, those that are more upright or mound-shaped, and those that scramble up into the lowest branches, like some of the hardy cranesbills. These will all thrive on the same cultivation regime as the shrubs. Use a good general fertilizer in spring, as recommended, and mulch annually.

**Right:** Arum italicum *lies dormant in summer, but during winter and early spring the patterned leaves make a good foil for snowdrops and other early-flowering bulbs. Both enjoy moist shade.*

**Below:** Helleborus orientalis *makes a good spring-flowering clump in dappled shade in a border or light woodland setting.*

# Carpet bedding

Carpet bedding was all the rage in Victorian gardens and today fashion-conscious gardeners everywhere are trying their hand at recreating antique flower beds. The essence of carpet bedding is to plant low-growing annuals close together to form patterns like a living Persian rug. You can use flowers or foliage or a mixture of both. The Victorians also created raised beds using wall-to-wall succulent plants. Many modern interpretations of the carpet bedding theme are in use around the world. One garden in Canada features life-size crinoline ladies, whose skirts are made from mounds of soil planted with *Impatiens*. They have wire torsos growing trailing ivy and are topped by genuine sun bonnets.

Choose plants that stay short and compact for carpet bedding schemes. One of the best compact foliage plants is *Alternanthera ficoidea amoena*, a half-hardy plant available in various foliage colors. Clip it regularly to keep plants tidy and to prevent them flowering. It is propagated from cuttings. You can achieve a similar effect using a dark-leaved lobelia, some kinds of *Amaranthus* or *Iresine* (bloodleaf). *Echeveria glauca*, a succulent plant with waxy blue leaves, is another popular foliage plant for carpet bedding. For flowering plants, choose almost any compact flowering annual: lobelia, alyssum, salvia, ageratum, etc. And as an authentic period piece, plunge a striking 'dot' plant - a symmetrically shaped plant, such as agave, yucca, cordyline or chusan palm - still in its pot, into the center of the bed. For a carpet bedding scheme to succeed, it is essential to plant in a soil that is totally free of perennial weeds. Deal with annual weeds immediately to avoid spoiling the pattern. Construct a 'bridge' over the bed - perhaps a plank raised up on bricks at each end - that allows you to weed without trampling over the plants.

*Above: Formal beds outlined in dwarf box, with large patterns created in red and pink busy lizzie (Impatiens) and silver senecio (Senecio bicolor cineraria).*

*In cold climates, the succulents in this scheme are frost tender. Keep the plants in heated conditions from fall to late spring to avoid expensive losses.*

**Above:** *An elaborate Victorian-style carpet bedding scheme needs a great deal of maintenance. A bed like this will have to be weeded every week.*

**Left:** *This formal Victorian-style carpet bedding scheme uses only foliage plants (*Echeveria glauca, Alternanthera *and* Sedum) *with a large variegated* Agave americana *as a dot plant in the center.*

**Right:** *This is a much more intricate Victorian-style pattern that combines* Echeveria glauca *with two kinds of* Amaranthus, *golden feverfew and flowering* Ageratum.

Ageratum

Golden feverfew

Amaranthus

Echeveria glauca

**Right:** *Here, feverfew and French marigolds are combined to make a delightful formal garden.*

103

# Subtropical bedding

The Victorians often made subtropical borders with annual bedding plants set out in rows and tall, striking 'dot' plants, such as canna or standard fuchsia, standing over them in the center of the bed. Foliage plants, such as cordyline palm or castor-oil plant, were used as dot plants to contrast with the flowers beneath. Later on, plants were also used more informally, with large-leaved foliage plants grouped together with exotic flowers for a jungly impression. This type of display looks good on a patio using plants in pots. Plants with good flowers and large leaves, such as canna cultivars with bronze-purple leaves, are specially useful if you do not have room for many plants. In a garden with striking large-leaved evergreens, add pot-grown exotic flowers for a summer display. When planning a subtropical display, consider what to do with the plants in winter. Most subtropical-look flowers will need to be kept in a frost-free conservatory, sunroom or greenhouse. (Prune shrubby daturas and salvias hard so that they take up less room.) Alternatively, stick to annuals, cheap perennials that are easily replaced each spring, and tuberous plants, such as canna and ginger lily, plus other summer-flowering bulbs (see page 48-49) that die down in winter.

page 48-49

*Below: A subtropical corner, with canna and Tithonia (Mexican zinnia) adding to the 'hot' colors of dahlias, sunflowers and red hot pokers. Chusan palm and eucalyptus foliage in the background add to the effect.*

**Suitable flowers**

Anigozanthos *(kangaroo paw)*
Argyranthemum
Begonia grandis evansiana
*(hardy in mild areas)*
Canna, *Castor-oil plant*
Datura *(also called* Brugmansia*)*
Gazania
Hedychium *(ginger lily)*
Heliotrope
*New Guinea hybrid* Impatiens
Osteospermum *(hardy in mild areas)*
*Shrubby salvias, e.g.*
Salvia fulgens, S. grahamii
*(hardy in mild areas)*

Cordyline australis 'Purpurea'

Coleus

Impatiens *(busy lizzie)*

Impatiens *New Guinea Hybrid*

104

Abutilon *hybrid. These elegant plants are not reliably hardy in cooler climates during the winter. Bring them into a frost-free environment and cut them back hard so that they take up less room.*

Argyranthemum foeniculaceum *(trained as a standard). This plant is frost-tender; bring it in or overwinter it as rooted cuttings (see page 22-23).*

Fatsia japonica. *These plants will survive outside during the winter, as long as you plunge the pots up to their rims in the soil in a sheltered spot.*

*x* Fatshedera lizei *'Variegata'. Overwinter this plant as for Fatsia.*

Echeveria

# Index to Plants

Page numbers in **bold** indicate major text references. Page numbers in *italics* indicate captions and annotations to photographs. Other text entries are shown in normal type.

# Credits

The majority of the photographs featured in this book have been taken by Neil Sutherland and are © Colour Library Books. The publishers wish to thank the following photographers for providing additional photographs, credited here by page number and position on the page, i.e. (B)Bottom, (T)Top, (C)Center, (BL)Bottom left, etc.

A-Z Botanical Photographic Collection: D.W. Bevan 27(CT), Michael R. Chandler 28(B)
Pat Brindley: 35(TR), 56(TR), 73(BR), 96
Eric Crichton: 28(TR), 32-3(B), 40(BR), 55(CL,BL), 72(BL,CB), 73(TR), 74(T), 76(BR), 79(TL), 93(BL), 103(T), 104(BL)
John Glover: Credits page, half title page, 15(BR), 29(TL,CR), 32(BL), 33(T), 39(BR), 41(BL), 52(R), 53(BL), 58(TR), 70, 70-1(T), 71(C,TR,BR), 79(R), 83(BR), 91(TR), 93(TR)
Natural Image: Bob Gibbons 78(L), Liz Gibbons 78(BR), Robin Fletcher 95(CL), Bob Gibbons 100(C)
Clive Nichols: 10, 11(Keukenhof Gardens), 19(CT, Designer Jill Billington), 29(BR), 32(TR), 33(R), 34(BL), 37(BR,CB), 39(CB), 42(BL), 43(TL,TC,TR), 51(BC,BR), 53(TR,BR), 54(L), 57(TL,TR) 58(BL), 59(CT,B), 60(BR), 62(BR), 73(L, Designer Wendy Francis), 74(BL), 74-5(CB), 75(TL,R), 78(TR), 81(TL,TR,BR) 88(TL), 89(TL,TR), 92(BR), 98(TR), 100-1(C), 101(BL,BR,CR), 102(B)
Photos Horticultural: 79(B), 83(TL)
Daan Smit: 53(TL)
Harry Smith Photographic Collection: 57(BR), 59(TR), 97(BR), 102(TR), 103(CB)
Don Wildridge: 52(BL)

## Acknowledgments

The publishers would like to thank Country Gardens at Chichester for providing plants and photographic facilities during the production of this book; thanks are particularly due to Cherry Burton and Sue Davey for their enthusiastic help and guidance.